A Day Book With Prompts

NIMBLE BOOKS LLC

Nimble Books LLC

1521 Martha Avenue

Ann Arbor, MI, USA 48103

http://www.NimbleBooks.com

wfz@nimblebooks.com

+1.734-330-2593

Version 1.0; last saved 2010-12-28.

Printed in the United States of America

ISBN-13: 978-1-60888-098-0

♾ The paper used in this publication meets the minimum requirements of the American National Standard for Information Sciences—Permanence of Paper for Printed Library Materials, ANSI Z39.48-1992. The paper is acid-free and lignin-free.

Month _____ Day ___ Year _____

Spiritual: pray, praise, serve ...

Family: love, listen, laugh ...

Friends: reach out, encourage, share ...

Morning rituals: shower, dress, breakfast ...

Vitals: weight, blood pressure, etc.

Medical: medicines, treatments, etc.

Food & nutrition: morning, afternoon, evening (with calories) ...

Exercise: flexibility, cardio, resistance, sports ...

Evening rituals: dinner, family, bed ...

To dos:

Delegated, postponed, declined:

Accomplishments

What, where, when, how, why, who was I today ...

Month _____ Day ___ Year _____

Spiritual: pray, praise, serve ...

Family: love, listen, laugh ...

Friends: reach out, encourage, share ...

Morning rituals: shower, dress, breakfast ...

Vitals: weight, blood pressure, etc.

Medical: medicines, treatments, etc.

Food & nutrition: morning, afternoon, evening (with calories) ...

Exercise: flexibility, cardio, resistance, sports ...

Evening rituals: dinner, family, bed ...

To dos:

Delegated, postponed, declined:

Accomplishments

What, where, when, how, why, who was I today ...

Month _____ Day ___ Year _____

Spiritual: pray, praise, serve ...

Family: love, listen, laugh ...

Friends: reach out, encourage, share ...

Morning rituals: shower, dress, breakfast ...

Vitals: weight, blood pressure, etc.

Medical: medicines, treatments, etc.

Food & nutrition: morning, afternoon, evening (with calories) ...

Exercise: flexibility, cardio, resistance, sports ...

Evening rituals: dinner, family, bed ...

To dos:

Delegated, postponed, declined:

Accomplishments

What, where, when, how, why, who was I today ...

Month _____ Day ___ Year _____

Spiritual: pray, praise, serve ...

Family: love, listen, laugh ...

Friends: reach out, encourage, share ...

Morning rituals: shower, dress, breakfast ...

Vitals: weight, blood pressure, etc.

Medical: medicines, treatments, etc.

Food & nutrition: morning, afternoon, evening (with calories) ...

Exercise: flexibility, cardio, resistance, sports ...

Evening rituals: dinner, family, bed ...

To dos:

Delegated, postponed, declined:

Accomplishments

What, where, when, how, why, who was I today ...

Month _____ Day ___ Year _____

Spiritual: pray, praise, serve ...

Family: love, listen, laugh ...

Friends: reach out, encourage, share ...

Morning rituals: shower, dress, breakfast ...

Vitals: weight, blood pressure, etc.

Medical: medicines, treatments, etc.

Food & nutrition: morning, afternoon, evening (with calories) ...

Exercise: flexibility, cardio, resistance, sports ...

Evening rituals: dinner, family, bed ...

To dos:

Delegated, postponed, declined:

Accomplishments

What, where, when, how, why, who was I today ...

Month _____ Day ___ Year _____

Spiritual: pray, praise, serve ...

Family: love, listen, laugh ...

Friends: reach out, encourage, share ...

Morning rituals: shower, dress, breakfast ...

Vitals: weight, blood pressure, etc.

Medical: medicines, treatments, etc.

Food & nutrition: morning, afternoon, evening (with calories) ...

Exercise: flexibility, cardio, resistance, sports ...

Evening rituals: dinner, family, bed ...

To dos:

Delegated, postponed, declined:

Accomplishments

What, where, when, how, why, who was I today ...

Month _____ Day ___ Year _____

Spiritual: pray, praise, serve ...

Family: love, listen, laugh ...

Friends: reach out, encourage, share ...

Morning rituals: shower, dress, breakfast ...

Vitals: weight, blood pressure, etc.

Medical: medicines, treatments, etc.

Food & nutrition: morning, afternoon, evening (with calories) ...

Exercise: flexibility, cardio, resistance, sports ...

Evening rituals: dinner, family, bed ...

To dos:

Delegated, postponed, declined:

Accomplishments

What, where, when, how, why, who was I today ...

Month _____ Day ___ Year _____

Spiritual: pray, praise, serve ...

Family: love, listen, laugh ...

Friends: reach out, encourage, share ...

Morning rituals: shower, dress, breakfast ...

Vitals: weight, blood pressure, etc.

Medical: medicines, treatments, etc.

Food & nutrition: morning, afternoon, evening (with calories) ...

Exercise: flexibility, cardio, resistance, sports ...

Evening rituals: dinner, family, bed ...

To dos:

Delegated, postponed, declined:

Accomplishments

What, where, when, how, why, who was I today ...

Month _____ Day ___ Year _____

Spiritual: pray, praise, serve ...

Family: love, listen, laugh ...

Friends: reach out, encourage, share ...

Morning rituals: shower, dress, breakfast ...

Vitals: weight, blood pressure, etc.

Medical: medicines, treatments, etc.

Food & nutrition: morning, afternoon, evening (with calories) ...

Exercise: flexibility, cardio, resistance, sports ...

Evening rituals: dinner, family, bed ...

To dos:

Delegated, postponed, declined:

Accomplishments

What, where, when, how, why, who was I today ...

Month _____ Day ___ Year _____

Spiritual: pray, praise, serve ...

Family: love, listen, laugh ...

Friends: reach out, encourage, share ...

Morning rituals: shower, dress, breakfast ...

Vitals: weight, blood pressure, etc.

Medical: medicines, treatments, etc.

Food & nutrition: morning, afternoon, evening (with calories) ...

Exercise: flexibility, cardio, resistance, sports ...

Evening rituals: dinner, family, bed ...

To dos:

Delegated, postponed, declined:

Accomplishments

What, where, when, how, why, who was I today ...

Month _____ Day ___ Year _____

Spiritual: pray, praise, serve ...

Family: love, listen, laugh ...

Friends: reach out, encourage, share ...

Morning rituals: shower, dress, breakfast ...

Vitals: weight, blood pressure, etc.

Medical: medicines, treatments, etc.

Food & nutrition: morning, afternoon, evening (with calories) ...

Exercise: flexibility, cardio, resistance, sports ...

Evening rituals: dinner, family, bed ...

To dos:

Delegated, postponed, declined:

Accomplishments

What, where, when, how, why, who was I today ...

Month _____ Day ___ Year _____

Spiritual: pray, praise, serve ...

Family: love, listen, laugh ...

Friends: reach out, encourage, share ...

Morning rituals: shower, dress, breakfast ...

Vitals: weight, blood pressure, etc.

Medical: medicines, treatments, etc.

Food & nutrition: morning, afternoon, evening (with calories) ...

Exercise: flexibility, cardio, resistance, sports ...

Evening rituals: dinner, family, bed ...

To dos:

Delegated, postponed, declined:

Accomplishments

What, where, when, how, why, who was I today ...

Month _____ Day ___ Year _____

Spiritual: pray, praise, serve ...

Family: love, listen, laugh ...

Friends: reach out, encourage, share ...

Morning rituals: shower, dress, breakfast ...

Vitals: weight, blood pressure, etc.

Medical: medicines, treatments, etc.

Food & nutrition: morning, afternoon, evening (with calories) ...

Exercise: flexibility, cardio, resistance, sports ...

Evening rituals: dinner, family, bed ...

To dos:

Delegated, postponed, declined:

Accomplishments

What, where, when, how, why, who was I today ...

Month _____ Day ___ Year _____

Spiritual: pray, praise, serve ...

Family: love, listen, laugh ...

Friends: reach out, encourage, share ...

Morning rituals: shower, dress, breakfast ...

Vitals: weight, blood pressure, etc.

Medical: medicines, treatments, etc.

Food & nutrition: morning, afternoon, evening (with calories) ...

Exercise: flexibility, cardio, resistance, sports ...

Evening rituals: dinner, family, bed ...

To dos:

Delegated, postponed, declined:

Accomplishments

What, where, when, how, why, who was I today ...

Month _____ Day ___ Year _____

Spiritual: pray, praise, serve ...

Family: love, listen, laugh ...

Friends: reach out, encourage, share ...

Morning rituals: shower, dress, breakfast ...

Vitals: weight, blood pressure, etc.

Medical: medicines, treatments, etc.

Food & nutrition: morning, afternoon, evening (with calories) ...

Exercise: flexibility, cardio, resistance, sports ...

Evening rituals: dinner, family, bed ...

To dos:

Delegated, postponed, declined:

Accomplishments

What, where, when, how, why, who was I today ...

Month _____ Day ___ Year _____

Spiritual: pray, praise, serve ...

Family: love, listen, laugh ...

Friends: reach out, encourage, share ...

Morning rituals: shower, dress, breakfast ...

Vitals: weight, blood pressure, etc.

Medical: medicines, treatments, etc.

Food & nutrition: morning, afternoon, evening (with calories) ...

Exercise: flexibility, cardio, resistance, sports ...

Evening rituals: dinner, family, bed ...

To dos:

Delegated, postponed, declined:

Accomplishments

What, where, when, how, why, who was I today ...

Month _____ Day ___ Year _____

Spiritual: pray, praise, serve ...

Family: love, listen, laugh ...

Friends: reach out, encourage, share ...

Morning rituals: shower, dress, breakfast ...

Vitals: weight, blood pressure, etc.

Medical: medicines, treatments, etc.

Food & nutrition: morning, afternoon, evening (with calories) ...

Exercise: flexibility, cardio, resistance, sports ...

Evening rituals: dinner, family, bed ...

To dos:

Delegated, postponed, declined:

Accomplishments

What, where, when, how, why, who was I today ...

Month _____ Day ___ Year _____

Spiritual: pray, praise, serve ...

Family: love, listen, laugh ...

Friends: reach out, encourage, share ...

Morning rituals: shower, dress, breakfast ...

Vitals: weight, blood pressure, etc.

Medical: medicines, treatments, etc.

Food & nutrition: morning, afternoon, evening (with calories) ...

Exercise: flexibility, cardio, resistance, sports ...

Evening rituals: dinner, family, bed ...

To dos:

Delegated, postponed, declined:

Accomplishments

What, where, when, how, why, who was I today ...

Month _____ Day ___ Year _____

Spiritual: pray, praise, serve ...

Family: love, listen, laugh ...

Friends: reach out, encourage, share ...

Morning rituals: shower, dress, breakfast ...

Vitals: weight, blood pressure, etc.

Medical: medicines, treatments, etc.

Food & nutrition: morning, afternoon, evening (with calories) ...

Exercise: flexibility, cardio, resistance, sports ...

Evening rituals: dinner, family, bed ...

To dos:

Delegated, postponed, declined:

Accomplishments

What, where, when, how, why, who was I today ...

Month _____ Day ___ Year _____

Spiritual: pray, praise, serve ...

Family: love, listen, laugh ...

Friends: reach out, encourage, share ...

Morning rituals: shower, dress, breakfast ...

Vitals: weight, blood pressure, etc.

Medical: medicines, treatments, etc.

Food & nutrition: morning, afternoon, evening (with calories) ...

Exercise: flexibility, cardio, resistance, sports ...

Evening rituals: dinner, family, bed ...

To dos:

Delegated, postponed, declined:

Accomplishments

What, where, when, how, why, who was I today ...

Month _____ Day ___ Year _____

Spiritual: pray, praise, serve ...

Family: love, listen, laugh ...

Friends: reach out, encourage, share ...

Morning rituals: shower, dress, breakfast ...

Vitals: weight, blood pressure, etc.

Medical: medicines, treatments, etc.

Food & nutrition: morning, afternoon, evening (with calories) ...

Exercise: flexibility, cardio, resistance, sports ...

Evening rituals: dinner, family, bed ...

To dos:

Delegated, postponed, declined:

Accomplishments

What, where, when, how, why, who was I today ...

Month _____ Day ___ Year _____

Spiritual: pray, praise, serve ...

Family: love, listen, laugh ...

Friends: reach out, encourage, share ...

Morning rituals: shower, dress, breakfast ...

Vitals: weight, blood pressure, etc.

Medical: medicines, treatments, etc.

Food & nutrition: morning, afternoon, evening (with calories) ...

Exercise: flexibility, cardio, resistance, sports ...

Evening rituals: dinner, family, bed ...

To dos:

Delegated, postponed, declined:

Accomplishments

What, where, when, how, why, who was I today ...

Spiritual: pray, praise, serve ...

Family: love, listen, laugh ...

Friends: reach out, encourage, share ...

Morning rituals: shower, dress, breakfast ...

Vitals: weight, blood pressure, etc.

Medical: medicines, treatments, etc.

Food & nutrition: morning, afternoon, evening (with calories) ...

Exercise: flexibility, cardio, resistance, sports ...

Evening rituals: dinner, family, bed ...

To dos:

Delegated, postponed, declined:

Accomplishments

What, where, when, how, why, who was I today ...

Month _____ Day ___ Year _____

Spiritual: pray, praise, serve ...

Family: love, listen, laugh ...

Friends: reach out, encourage, share ...

Morning rituals: shower, dress, breakfast ...

Vitals: weight, blood pressure, etc.

Medical: medicines, treatments, etc.

Food & nutrition: morning, afternoon, evening (with calories) ...

Exercise: flexibility, cardio, resistance, sports ...

Evening rituals: dinner, family, bed ...

To dos:

Delegated, postponed, declined:

Accomplishments

What, where, when, how, why, who was I today ...

Month _____ Day ___ Year _____

Spiritual: pray, praise, serve ...

Family: love, listen, laugh ...

Friends: reach out, encourage, share ...

Morning rituals: shower, dress, breakfast ...

Vitals: weight, blood pressure, etc.

Medical: medicines, treatments, etc.

Food & nutrition: morning, afternoon, evening (with calories) ...

Exercise: flexibility, cardio, resistance, sports ...

Evening rituals: dinner, family, bed ...

To dos:

Delegated, postponed, declined:

Accomplishments

What, where, when, how, why, who was I today ...

Month _____ Day ___ Year _____

Spiritual: pray, praise, serve ...

Family: love, listen, laugh ...

Friends: reach out, encourage, share ...

Morning rituals: shower, dress, breakfast ...

Vitals: weight, blood pressure, etc.

Medical: medicines, treatments, etc.

Food & nutrition: morning, afternoon, evening (with calories) ...

Exercise: flexibility, cardio, resistance, sports ...

Evening rituals: dinner, family, bed ...

To dos:

Delegated, postponed, declined:

Accomplishments

What, where, when, how, why, who was I today ...

Spiritual: pray, praise, serve ...

Family: love, listen, laugh ...

Friends: reach out, encourage, share ...

Morning rituals: shower, dress, breakfast ...

Vitals: weight, blood pressure, etc.

Medical: medicines, treatments, etc.

Food & nutrition: morning, afternoon, evening (with calories) ...

Exercise: flexibility, cardio, resistance, sports ...

Evening rituals: dinner, family, bed ...

To dos:

Delegated, postponed, declined:

Accomplishments

What, where, when, how, why, who was I today ...

Month _____ Day ___ Year _____

Spiritual: pray, praise, serve ...

Family: love, listen, laugh ...

Friends: reach out, encourage, share ...

Morning rituals: shower, dress, breakfast ...

Vitals: weight, blood pressure, etc.

Medical: medicines, treatments, etc.

Food & nutrition: morning, afternoon, evening (with calories) ...

Exercise: flexibility, cardio, resistance, sports ...

Evening rituals: dinner, family, bed ...

To dos:

Delegated, postponed, declined:

Accomplishments

What, where, when, how, why, who was I today ...

Spiritual: pray, praise, serve ...

Family: love, listen, laugh ...

Friends: reach out, encourage, share ...

Morning rituals: shower, dress, breakfast ...

Vitals: weight, blood pressure, etc.

Medical: medicines, treatments, etc.

Food & nutrition: morning, afternoon, evening (with calories) ...

Exercise: flexibility, cardio, resistance, sports ...

Evening rituals: dinner, family, bed ...

To dos:

Delegated, postponed, declined:

Accomplishments

What, where, when, how, why, who was I today ...

Month _____ Day ___ Year _____

Spiritual: pray, praise, serve ...

Family: love, listen, laugh ...

Friends: reach out, encourage, share ...

Morning rituals: shower, dress, breakfast ...

Vitals: weight, blood pressure, etc.

Medical: medicines, treatments, etc.

Food & nutrition: morning, afternoon, evening (with calories) ...

Exercise: flexibility, cardio, resistance, sports ...

Evening rituals: dinner, family, bed ...

To dos:

Delegated, postponed, declined:

Accomplishments

What, where, when, how, why, who was I today ...

Month _____ Day ___ Year _____

Spiritual: pray, praise, serve ...

Family: love, listen, laugh ...

Friends: reach out, encourage, share ...

Morning rituals: shower, dress, breakfast ...

Vitals: weight, blood pressure, etc.

Medical: medicines, treatments, etc.

Food & nutrition: morning, afternoon, evening (with calories) ...

Exercise: flexibility, cardio, resistance, sports ...

Evening rituals: dinner, family, bed ...

To dos:

Delegated, postponed, declined:

Accomplishments

What, where, when, how, why, who was I today ...

Month _____ Day ___ Year _____

Spiritual: pray, praise, serve ...

Family: love, listen, laugh ...

Friends: reach out, encourage, share ...

Morning rituals: shower, dress, breakfast ...

Vitals: weight, blood pressure, etc.

Medical: medicines, treatments, etc.

Food & nutrition: morning, afternoon, evening (with calories) ...

Exercise: flexibility, cardio, resistance, sports ...

Evening rituals: dinner, family, bed ...

To dos:

Delegated, postponed, declined:

Accomplishments

What, where, when, how, why, who was I today ...

Spiritual: pray, praise, serve ...

Family: love, listen, laugh ...

Friends: reach out, encourage, share ...

Morning rituals: shower, dress, breakfast ...

Vitals: weight, blood pressure, etc.

Medical: medicines, treatments, etc.

Food & nutrition: morning, afternoon, evening (with calories) ...

Exercise: flexibility, cardio, resistance, sports ...

Evening rituals: dinner, family, bed ...

To dos:

Delegated, postponed, declined:

Accomplishments

What, where, when, how, why, who was I today ...

Month _____ Day ___ Year _____

Spiritual: pray, praise, serve ...

Family: love, listen, laugh ...

Friends: reach out, encourage, share ...

Morning rituals: shower, dress, breakfast ...

Vitals: weight, blood pressure, etc.

Medical: medicines, treatments, etc.

Food & nutrition: morning, afternoon, evening (with calories) ...

Exercise: flexibility, cardio, resistance, sports ...

Evening rituals: dinner, family, bed ...

To dos:

Delegated, postponed, declined:

Accomplishments

What, where, when, how, why, who was I today ...

Month _____ Day ___ Year _____

Spiritual: pray, praise, serve ...

Family: love, listen, laugh ...

Friends: reach out, encourage, share ...

Morning rituals: shower, dress, breakfast ...

Vitals: weight, blood pressure, etc.

Medical: medicines, treatments, etc.

Food & nutrition: morning, afternoon, evening (with calories) ...

Exercise: flexibility, cardio, resistance, sports ...

Evening rituals: dinner, family, bed ...

To dos:

Delegated, postponed, declined:

Accomplishments

What, where, when, how, why, who was I today ...

Month _____ Day ___ Year _____

Spiritual: pray, praise, serve ...

Family: love, listen, laugh ...

Friends: reach out, encourage, share ...

Morning rituals: shower, dress, breakfast ...

Vitals: weight, blood pressure, etc.

Medical: medicines, treatments, etc.

Food & nutrition: morning, afternoon, evening (with calories) ...

Exercise: flexibility, cardio, resistance, sports ...

Evening rituals: dinner, family, bed ...

To dos:

Delegated, postponed, declined:

Accomplishments

What, where, when, how, why, who was I today ...

Spiritual: pray, praise, serve ...

Family: love, listen, laugh ...

Friends: reach out, encourage, share ...

Morning rituals: shower, dress, breakfast ...

Vitals: weight, blood pressure, etc.

Medical: medicines, treatments, etc.

Food & nutrition: morning, afternoon, evening (with calories) ...

Exercise: flexibility, cardio, resistance, sports ...

Evening rituals: dinner, family, bed ...

To dos:

Delegated, postponed, declined:

Accomplishments

What, where, when, how, why, who was I today ...

Month _____ Day ___ Year _____

Spiritual: pray, praise, serve ...

Family: love, listen, laugh ...

Friends: reach out, encourage, share ...

Morning rituals: shower, dress, breakfast ...

Vitals: weight, blood pressure, etc.

Medical: medicines, treatments, etc.

Food & nutrition: morning, afternoon, evening (with calories) ...

Exercise: flexibility, cardio, resistance, sports ...

Evening rituals: dinner, family, bed ...

To dos:

Delegated, postponed, declined:

Accomplishments

What, where, when, how, why, who was I today ...

Month _____ Day ___ Year _____

Spiritual: pray, praise, serve ...

Family: love, listen, laugh ...

Friends: reach out, encourage, share ...

Morning rituals: shower, dress, breakfast ...

Vitals: weight, blood pressure, etc.

Medical: medicines, treatments, etc.

Food & nutrition: morning, afternoon, evening (with calories) ...

Exercise: flexibility, cardio, resistance, sports ...

Evening rituals: dinner, family, bed ...

To dos:

Delegated, postponed, declined:

Accomplishments

What, where, when, how, why, who was I today ...

Month _____ Day ___ Year _____

Spiritual: pray, praise, serve ...

Family: love, listen, laugh ...

Friends: reach out, encourage, share ...

Morning rituals: shower, dress, breakfast ...

Vitals: weight, blood pressure, etc.

Medical: medicines, treatments, etc.

Food & nutrition: morning, afternoon, evening (with calories) ...

Exercise: flexibility, cardio, resistance, sports ...

Evening rituals: dinner, family, bed ...

To dos:

Delegated, postponed, declined:

Accomplishments

What, where, when, how, why, who was I today ...

Month _____ Day ___ Year _____

Spiritual: pray, praise, serve ...

Family: love, listen, laugh ...

Friends: reach out, encourage, share ...

Morning rituals: shower, dress, breakfast ...

Vitals: weight, blood pressure, etc.

Medical: medicines, treatments, etc.

Food & nutrition: morning, afternoon, evening (with calories) ...

Exercise: flexibility, cardio, resistance, sports ...

Evening rituals: dinner, family, bed ...

To dos:

Delegated, postponed, declined:

Accomplishments

What, where, when, how, why, who was I today ...

Month _____ Day ___ Year _____

Spiritual: pray, praise, serve ...

Family: love, listen, laugh ...

Friends: reach out, encourage, share ...

Morning rituals: shower, dress, breakfast ...

Vitals: weight, blood pressure, etc.

Medical: medicines, treatments, etc.

Food & nutrition: morning, afternoon, evening (with calories) ...

Exercise: flexibility, cardio, resistance, sports ...

Evening rituals: dinner, family, bed ...

To dos:

Delegated, postponed, declined:

Accomplishments

What, where, when, how, why, who was I today ...

Month _____ Day ____ Year _____

Spiritual: pray, praise, serve ...

Family: love, listen, laugh ...

Friends: reach out, encourage, share ...

Morning rituals: shower, dress, breakfast ...

Vitals: weight, blood pressure, etc.

Medical: medicines, treatments, etc.

Food & nutrition: morning, afternoon, evening (with calories) ...

Exercise: flexibility, cardio, resistance, sports ...

Evening rituals: dinner, family, bed ...

To dos:

Delegated, postponed, declined:

Accomplishments

What, where, when, how, why, who was I today ...

Month _____ Day ___ Year _____

Spiritual: pray, praise, serve ...

Family: love, listen, laugh ...

Friends: reach out, encourage, share ...

Morning rituals: shower, dress, breakfast ...

Vitals: weight, blood pressure, etc.

Medical: medicines, treatments, etc.

Food & nutrition: morning, afternoon, evening (with calories) ...

Exercise: flexibility, cardio, resistance, sports ...

Evening rituals: dinner, family, bed ...

To dos:

Delegated, postponed, declined:

Accomplishments

What, where, when, how, why, who was I today ...

Month _____ Day ___ Year _____

Spiritual: pray, praise, serve ...

Family: love, listen, laugh ...

Friends: reach out, encourage, share ...

Morning rituals: shower, dress, breakfast ...

Vitals: weight, blood pressure, etc.

Medical: medicines, treatments, etc.

Food & nutrition: morning, afternoon, evening (with calories) ...

Exercise: flexibility, cardio, resistance, sports ...

Evening rituals: dinner, family, bed ...

To dos:

Delegated, postponed, declined:

Accomplishments

What, where, when, how, why, who was I today ...

Month _____ Day ___ Year _____

Spiritual: pray, praise, serve ...

Family: love, listen, laugh ...

Friends: reach out, encourage, share ...

Morning rituals: shower, dress, breakfast ...

Vitals: weight, blood pressure, etc.

Medical: medicines, treatments, etc.

Food & nutrition: morning, afternoon, evening (with calories) ...

Exercise: flexibility, cardio, resistance, sports ...

Evening rituals: dinner, family, bed ...

To dos:

Delegated, postponed, declined:

Accomplishments

What, where, when, how, why, who was I today ...

Spiritual: pray, praise, serve ...

Family: love, listen, laugh ...

Friends: reach out, encourage, share ...

Morning rituals: shower, dress, breakfast ...

Vitals: weight, blood pressure, etc.

Medical: medicines, treatments, etc.

Food & nutrition: morning, afternoon, evening (with calories) ...

Exercise: flexibility, cardio, resistance, sports ...

Evening rituals: dinner, family, bed ...

To dos:

Delegated, postponed, declined:

Accomplishments

What, where, when, how, why, who was I today ...

Month _____ Day ___ Year _____

Spiritual: pray, praise, serve ...

Family: love, listen, laugh ...

Friends: reach out, encourage, share ...

Morning rituals: shower, dress, breakfast ...

Vitals: weight, blood pressure, etc.

Medical: medicines, treatments, etc.

Food & nutrition: morning, afternoon, evening (with calories) ...

Exercise: flexibility, cardio, resistance, sports ...

Evening rituals: dinner, family, bed ...

To dos:

Delegated, postponed, declined:

Accomplishments

What, where, when, how, why, who was I today ...

Spiritual: pray, praise, serve ...

Family: love, listen, laugh ...

Friends: reach out, encourage, share ...

Morning rituals: shower, dress, breakfast ...

Vitals: weight, blood pressure, etc.

Medical: medicines, treatments, etc.

Food & nutrition: morning, afternoon, evening (with calories) ...

Exercise: flexibility, cardio, resistance, sports ...

Evening rituals: dinner, family, bed ...

To dos:

Delegated, postponed, declined:

Accomplishments

What, where, when, how, why, who was I today ...

Month _____ Day ___ Year _____

Spiritual: pray, praise, serve ...

Family: love, listen, laugh ...

Friends: reach out, encourage, share ...

Morning rituals: shower, dress, breakfast ...

Vitals: weight, blood pressure, etc.

Medical: medicines, treatments, etc.

Food & nutrition: morning, afternoon, evening (with calories) ...

Exercise: flexibility, cardio, resistance, sports ...

Evening rituals: dinner, family, bed ...

To dos:

Delegated, postponed, declined:

Accomplishments

What, where, when, how, why, who was I today ...

Month _____ Day ___ Year _____

Spiritual: pray, praise, serve ...

Family: love, listen, laugh ...

Friends: reach out, encourage, share ...

Morning rituals: shower, dress, breakfast ...

Vitals: weight, blood pressure, etc.

Medical: medicines, treatments, etc.

Food & nutrition: morning, afternoon, evening (with calories) ...

Exercise: flexibility, cardio, resistance, sports ...

Evening rituals: dinner, family, bed ...

To dos:

Delegated, postponed, declined:

Accomplishments

What, where, when, how, why, who was I today ...

Month _____ Day ___ Year _____

Spiritual: pray, praise, serve ...

Family: love, listen, laugh ...

Friends: reach out, encourage, share ...

Morning rituals: shower, dress, breakfast ...

Vitals: weight, blood pressure, etc.

Medical: medicines, treatments, etc.

Food & nutrition: morning, afternoon, evening (with calories) ...

Exercise: flexibility, cardio, resistance, sports ...

Evening rituals: dinner, family, bed ...

To dos:

Delegated, postponed, declined:

Accomplishments

What, where, when, how, why, who was I today ...

Month _____ Day ___ Year _____

Spiritual: pray, praise, serve ...

Family: love, listen, laugh ...

Friends: reach out, encourage, share ...

Morning rituals: shower, dress, breakfast ...

Vitals: weight, blood pressure, etc.

Medical: medicines, treatments, etc.

Food & nutrition: morning, afternoon, evening (with calories) ...

Exercise: flexibility, cardio, resistance, sports ...

Evening rituals: dinner, family, bed ...

To dos:

Delegated, postponed, declined:

Accomplishments

What, where, when, how, why, who was I today ...

Month _____ Day ___ Year _____

Spiritual: pray, praise, serve ...

Family: love, listen, laugh ...

Friends: reach out, encourage, share ...

Morning rituals: shower, dress, breakfast ...

Vitals: weight, blood pressure, etc.

Medical: medicines, treatments, etc.

Food & nutrition: morning, afternoon, evening (with calories) ...

Exercise: flexibility, cardio, resistance, sports ...

Evening rituals: dinner, family, bed ...

To dos:

Delegated, postponed, declined:

Accomplishments

What, where, when, how, why, who was I today ...

Month _____ Day ___ Year _____

Spiritual: pray, praise, serve ...

Family: love, listen, laugh ...

Friends: reach out, encourage, share ...

Morning rituals: shower, dress, breakfast ...

Vitals: weight, blood pressure, etc.

Medical: medicines, treatments, etc.

Food & nutrition: morning, afternoon, evening (with calories) ...

Exercise: flexibility, cardio, resistance, sports ...

Evening rituals: dinner, family, bed ...

To dos:

Delegated, postponed, declined:

Accomplishments

What, where, when, how, why, who was I today ...

Month _____ Day ___ Year _____

Spiritual: pray, praise, serve ...

Family: love, listen, laugh ...

Friends: reach out, encourage, share ...

Morning rituals: shower, dress, breakfast ...

Vitals: weight, blood pressure, etc.

Medical: medicines, treatments, etc.

Food & nutrition: morning, afternoon, evening (with calories) ...

Exercise: flexibility, cardio, resistance, sports ...

Evening rituals: dinner, family, bed ...

To dos:

Delegated, postponed, declined:

Accomplishments

What, where, when, how, why, who was I today ...

Month _____ Day ___ Year _____

Spiritual: pray, praise, serve ...

Family: love, listen, laugh ...

Friends: reach out, encourage, share ...

Morning rituals: shower, dress, breakfast ...

Vitals: weight, blood pressure, etc.

Medical: medicines, treatments, etc.

Food & nutrition: morning, afternoon, evening (with calories) ...

Exercise: flexibility, cardio, resistance, sports ...

Evening rituals: dinner, family, bed ...

To dos:

Delegated, postponed, declined:

Accomplishments

What, where, when, how, why, who was I today ...

Month _____ Day ___ Year _____

Spiritual: pray, praise, serve ...

Family: love, listen, laugh ...

Friends: reach out, encourage, share ...

Morning rituals: shower, dress, breakfast ...

Vitals: weight, blood pressure, etc.

Medical: medicines, treatments, etc.

Food & nutrition: morning, afternoon, evening (with calories) ...

Exercise: flexibility, cardio, resistance, sports ...

Evening rituals: dinner, family, bed ...

To dos:

Delegated, postponed, declined:

Accomplishments

What, where, when, how, why, who was I today ...

Month _____ Day ___ Year _____

Spiritual: pray, praise, serve ...

Family: love, listen, laugh ...

Friends: reach out, encourage, share ...

Morning rituals: shower, dress, breakfast ...

Vitals: weight, blood pressure, etc.

Medical: medicines, treatments, etc.

Food & nutrition: morning, afternoon, evening (with calories) ...

Exercise: flexibility, cardio, resistance, sports ...

Evening rituals: dinner, family, bed ...

To dos:

Delegated, postponed, declined:

Accomplishments

What, where, when, how, why, who was I today ...

Month _____ Day ___ Year _____

Spiritual: pray, praise, serve ...

Family: love, listen, laugh ...

Friends: reach out, encourage, share ...

Morning rituals: shower, dress, breakfast ...

Vitals: weight, blood pressure, etc.

Medical: medicines, treatments, etc.

Food & nutrition: morning, afternoon, evening (with calories) ...

Exercise: flexibility, cardio, resistance, sports ...

Evening rituals: dinner, family, bed ...

To dos:

Delegated, postponed, declined:

Accomplishments

What, where, when, how, why, who was I today ...

Month _____ Day ___ Year _____

Spiritual: pray, praise, serve ...

Family: love, listen, laugh ...

Friends: reach out, encourage, share ...

Morning rituals: shower, dress, breakfast ...

Vitals: weight, blood pressure, etc.

Medical: medicines, treatments, etc.

Food & nutrition: morning, afternoon, evening (with calories) ...

Exercise: flexibility, cardio, resistance, sports ...

Evening rituals: dinner, family, bed ...

To dos:

Delegated, postponed, declined:

Accomplishments

What, where, when, how, why, who was I today ...

Month _____ Day ___ Year _____

Spiritual: pray, praise, serve ...

Family: love, listen, laugh ...

Friends: reach out, encourage, share ...

Morning rituals: shower, dress, breakfast ...

Vitals: weight, blood pressure, etc.

Medical: medicines, treatments, etc.

Food & nutrition: morning, afternoon, evening (with calories) ...

Exercise: flexibility, cardio, resistance, sports ...

Evening rituals: dinner, family, bed ...

To dos:

Delegated, postponed, declined:

Accomplishments

What, where, when, how, why, who was I today ...

Month _____ Day ___ Year _____

Spiritual: pray, praise, serve ...

Family: love, listen, laugh ...

Friends: reach out, encourage, share ...

Morning rituals: shower, dress, breakfast ...

Vitals: weight, blood pressure, etc.

Medical: medicines, treatments, etc.

Food & nutrition: morning, afternoon, evening (with calories) ...

Exercise: flexibility, cardio, resistance, sports ...

Evening rituals: dinner, family, bed ...

To dos:

Delegated, postponed, declined:

Accomplishments

What, where, when, how, why, who was I today ...

Month _____ Day ___ Year _____

Spiritual: pray, praise, serve ...

Family: love, listen, laugh ...

Friends: reach out, encourage, share ...

Morning rituals: shower, dress, breakfast ...

Vitals: weight, blood pressure, etc.

Medical: medicines, treatments, etc.

Food & nutrition: morning, afternoon, evening (with calories) ...

Exercise: flexibility, cardio, resistance, sports ...

Evening rituals: dinner, family, bed ...

To dos:

Delegated, postponed, declined:

Accomplishments

What, where, when, how, why, who was I today ...

Month _____ Day ___ Year _____

Spiritual: pray, praise, serve ...

Family: love, listen, laugh ...

Friends: reach out, encourage, share ...

Morning rituals: shower, dress, breakfast ...

Vitals: weight, blood pressure, etc.

Medical: medicines, treatments, etc.

Food & nutrition: morning, afternoon, evening (with calories) ...

Exercise: flexibility, cardio, resistance, sports ...

Evening rituals: dinner, family, bed ...

To dos:

Delegated, postponed, declined:

Accomplishments

What, where, when, how, why, who was I today ...

Month _____ Day ___ Year _____

Spiritual: pray, praise, serve ...

Family: love, listen, laugh ...

Friends: reach out, encourage, share ...

Morning rituals: shower, dress, breakfast ...

Vitals: weight, blood pressure, etc.

Medical: medicines, treatments, etc.

Food & nutrition: morning, afternoon, evening (with calories) ...

Exercise: flexibility, cardio, resistance, sports ...

Evening rituals: dinner, family, bed ...

To dos:

Delegated, postponed, declined:

Accomplishments

What, where, when, how, why, who was I today ...

Month _____ Day ___ Year _____

Spiritual: pray, praise, serve ...

Family: love, listen, laugh ...

Friends: reach out, encourage, share ...

Morning rituals: shower, dress, breakfast ...

Vitals: weight, blood pressure, etc.

Medical: medicines, treatments, etc.

Food & nutrition: morning, afternoon, evening (with calories) ...

Exercise: flexibility, cardio, resistance, sports ...

Evening rituals: dinner, family, bed ...

To dos:

Delegated, postponed, declined:

Accomplishments

What, where, when, how, why, who was I today ...

Month _____ Day ___ Year _____

Spiritual: pray, praise, serve ...

Family: love, listen, laugh ...

Friends: reach out, encourage, share ...

Morning rituals: shower, dress, breakfast ...

Vitals: weight, blood pressure, etc.

Medical: medicines, treatments, etc.

Food & nutrition: morning, afternoon, evening (with calories) ...

Exercise: flexibility, cardio, resistance, sports ...

Evening rituals: dinner, family, bed ...

To dos:

Delegated, postponed, declined:

Accomplishments

What, where, when, how, why, who was I today ...

Spiritual: pray, praise, serve ...

Family: love, listen, laugh ...

Friends: reach out, encourage, share ...

Morning rituals: shower, dress, breakfast ...

Vitals: weight, blood pressure, etc.

Medical: medicines, treatments, etc.

Food & nutrition: morning, afternoon, evening (with calories) ...

Exercise: flexibility, cardio, resistance, sports ...

Evening rituals: dinner, family, bed ...

To dos:

Delegated, postponed, declined:

Accomplishments

What, where, when, how, why, who was I today ...

Month _____ Day ___ Year _____

Spiritual: pray, praise, serve ...

Family: love, listen, laugh ...

Friends: reach out, encourage, share ...

Morning rituals: shower, dress, breakfast ...

Vitals: weight, blood pressure, etc.

Medical: medicines, treatments, etc.

Food & nutrition: morning, afternoon, evening (with calories) ...

Exercise: flexibility, cardio, resistance, sports ...

Evening rituals: dinner, family, bed ...

To dos:

Delegated, postponed, declined:

Accomplishments

What, where, when, how, why, who was I today ...

Month _____ Day ___ Year _____

Spiritual: pray, praise, serve ...

Family: love, listen, laugh ...

Friends: reach out, encourage, share ...

Morning rituals: shower, dress, breakfast ...

Vitals: weight, blood pressure, etc.

Medical: medicines, treatments, etc.

Food & nutrition: morning, afternoon, evening (with calories) ...

Exercise: flexibility, cardio, resistance, sports ...

Evening rituals: dinner, family, bed ...

To dos:

Delegated, postponed, declined:

Accomplishments

What, where, when, how, why, who was I today ...

Month _____ Day ___ Year _____

Spiritual: pray, praise, serve ...

Family: love, listen, laugh ...

Friends: reach out, encourage, share ...

Morning rituals: shower, dress, breakfast ...

Vitals: weight, blood pressure, etc.

Medical: medicines, treatments, etc.

Food & nutrition: morning, afternoon, evening (with calories) ...

Exercise: flexibility, cardio, resistance, sports ...

Evening rituals: dinner, family, bed ...

To dos:

Delegated, postponed, declined:

Accomplishments

What, where, when, how, why, who was I today ...

Spiritual: pray, praise, serve ...

Family: love, listen, laugh ...

Friends: reach out, encourage, share ...

Morning rituals: shower, dress, breakfast ...

Vitals: weight, blood pressure, etc.

Medical: medicines, treatments, etc.

Food & nutrition: morning, afternoon, evening (with calories) ...

Exercise: flexibility, cardio, resistance, sports ...

Evening rituals: dinner, family, bed ...

To dos:

Delegated, postponed, declined:

Accomplishments

What, where, when, how, why, who was I today ...

Month _____ Day ____ Year _____

Spiritual: pray, praise, serve ...

Family: love, listen, laugh ...

Friends: reach out, encourage, share ...

Morning rituals: shower, dress, breakfast ...

Vitals: weight, blood pressure, etc.

Medical: medicines, treatments, etc.

Food & nutrition: morning, afternoon, evening (with calories) ...

Exercise: flexibility, cardio, resistance, sports ...

Evening rituals: dinner, family, bed ...

To dos:

Delegated, postponed, declined:

Accomplishments

What, where, when, how, why, who was I today ...

Month _____ Day ___ Year _____

Spiritual: pray, praise, serve ...

Family: love, listen, laugh ...

Friends: reach out, encourage, share ...

Morning rituals: shower, dress, breakfast ...

Vitals: weight, blood pressure, etc.

Medical: medicines, treatments, etc.

Food & nutrition: morning, afternoon, evening (with calories) ...

Exercise: flexibility, cardio, resistance, sports ...

Evening rituals: dinner, family, bed ...

To dos:

Delegated, postponed, declined:

Accomplishments

What, where, when, how, why, who was I today ...

Month _____ Day ___ Year _____

Spiritual: pray, praise, serve ...

Family: love, listen, laugh ...

Friends: reach out, encourage, share ...

Morning rituals: shower, dress, breakfast ...

Vitals: weight, blood pressure, etc.

Medical: medicines, treatments, etc.

Food & nutrition: morning, afternoon, evening (with calories) ...

Exercise: flexibility, cardio, resistance, sports ...

Evening rituals: dinner, family, bed ...

To dos:

Delegated, postponed, declined:

Accomplishments

What, where, when, how, why, who was I today ...

Spiritual: pray, praise, serve ...

Family: love, listen, laugh ...

Friends: reach out, encourage, share ...

Morning rituals: shower, dress, breakfast ...

Vitals: weight, blood pressure, etc.

Medical: medicines, treatments, etc.

Food & nutrition: morning, afternoon, evening (with calories) ...

Exercise: flexibility, cardio, resistance, sports ...

Evening rituals: dinner, family, bed ...

To dos:

Delegated, postponed, declined:

Accomplishments

What, where, when, how, why, who was I today ...

Month _____ Day ___ Year _____

Spiritual: pray, praise, serve ...

Family: love, listen, laugh ...

Friends: reach out, encourage, share ...

Morning rituals: shower, dress, breakfast ...

Vitals: weight, blood pressure, etc.

Medical: medicines, treatments, etc.

Food & nutrition: morning, afternoon, evening (with calories) ...

Exercise: flexibility, cardio, resistance, sports ...

Evening rituals: dinner, family, bed ...

To dos:

Delegated, postponed, declined:

Accomplishments

What, where, when, how, why, who was I today ...

Spiritual: pray, praise, serve ...

Family: love, listen, laugh ...

Friends: reach out, encourage, share ...

Morning rituals: shower, dress, breakfast ...

Vitals: weight, blood pressure, etc.

Medical: medicines, treatments, etc.

Food & nutrition: morning, afternoon, evening (with calories) ...

Exercise: flexibility, cardio, resistance, sports ...

Evening rituals: dinner, family, bed ...

To dos:

Delegated, postponed, declined:

Accomplishments

What, where, when, how, why, who was I today ...

Month _____ Day ___ Year _____

Spiritual: pray, praise, serve ...

Family: love, listen, laugh ...

Friends: reach out, encourage, share ...

Morning rituals: shower, dress, breakfast ...

Vitals: weight, blood pressure, etc.

Medical: medicines, treatments, etc.

Food & nutrition: morning, afternoon, evening (with calories) ...

Exercise: flexibility, cardio, resistance, sports ...

Evening rituals: dinner, family, bed ...

To dos:

Delegated, postponed, declined:

Accomplishments

What, where, when, how, why, who was I today ...

Month _____ Day ___ Year _____

Spiritual: pray, praise, serve ...

Family: love, listen, laugh ...

Friends: reach out, encourage, share ...

Morning rituals: shower, dress, breakfast ...

Vitals: weight, blood pressure, etc.

Medical: medicines, treatments, etc.

Food & nutrition: morning, afternoon, evening (with calories) ...

Exercise: flexibility, cardio, resistance, sports ...

Evening rituals: dinner, family, bed ...

To dos:

Delegated, postponed, declined:

Accomplishments

What, where, when, how, why, who was I today ...

Month _____ Day ___ Year _____

Spiritual: pray, praise, serve ...

Family: love, listen, laugh ...

Friends: reach out, encourage, share ...

Morning rituals: shower, dress, breakfast ...

Vitals: weight, blood pressure, etc.

Medical: medicines, treatments, etc.

Food & nutrition: morning, afternoon, evening (with calories) ...

Exercise: flexibility, cardio, resistance, sports ...

Evening rituals: dinner, family, bed ...

To dos:

Delegated, postponed, declined:

Accomplishments

What, where, when, how, why, who was I today ...

Spiritual: pray, praise, serve ...

Family: love, listen, laugh ...

Friends: reach out, encourage, share ...

Morning rituals: shower, dress, breakfast ...

Vitals: weight, blood pressure, etc.

Medical: medicines, treatments, etc.

Food & nutrition: morning, afternoon, evening (with calories) ...

Exercise: flexibility, cardio, resistance, sports ...

Evening rituals: dinner, family, bed ...

To dos:

Delegated, postponed, declined:

Accomplishments

What, where, when, how, why, who was I today ...

Month _____ Day ___ Year _____

Spiritual: pray, praise, serve ...

Family: love, listen, laugh ...

Friends: reach out, encourage, share ...

Morning rituals: shower, dress, breakfast ...

Vitals: weight, blood pressure, etc.

Medical: medicines, treatments, etc.

Food & nutrition: morning, afternoon, evening (with calories) ...

Exercise: flexibility, cardio, resistance, sports ...

Evening rituals: dinner, family, bed ...

To dos:

Delegated, postponed, declined:

Accomplishments

What, where, when, how, why, who was I today ...

Month _____ Day ____ Year _____

Spiritual: pray, praise, serve ...

Family: love, listen, laugh ...

Friends: reach out, encourage, share ...

Morning rituals: shower, dress, breakfast ...

Vitals: weight, blood pressure, etc.

Medical: medicines, treatments, etc.

Food & nutrition: morning, afternoon, evening (with calories) ...

Exercise: flexibility, cardio, resistance, sports ...

Evening rituals: dinner, family, bed ...

To dos:

Delegated, postponed, declined:

Accomplishments

What, where, when, how, why, who was 1 today ...

Month _____ Day ___ Year _____

Spiritual: pray, praise, serve ...

Family: love, listen, laugh ...

Friends: reach out, encourage, share ...

Morning rituals: shower, dress, breakfast ...

Vitals: weight, blood pressure, etc.

Medical: medicines, treatments, etc.

Food & nutrition: morning, afternoon, evening (with calories) ...

Exercise: flexibility, cardio, resistance, sports ...

Evening rituals: dinner, family, bed ...

To dos:

Delegated, postponed, declined:

Accomplishments

What, where, when, how, why, who was I today ...

Spiritual: pray, praise, serve ...

Family: love, listen, laugh ...

Friends: reach out, encourage, share ...

Morning rituals: shower, dress, breakfast ...

Vitals: weight, blood pressure, etc.

Medical: medicines, treatments, etc.

Food & nutrition: morning, afternoon, evening (with calories) ...

Exercise: flexibility, cardio, resistance, sports ...

Evening rituals: dinner, family, bed ...

To dos:

Delegated, postponed, declined:

Accomplishments

What, where, when, how, why, who was I today ...

Month _____ Day ___ Year _____

Spiritual: pray, praise, serve ...

Family: love, listen, laugh ...

Friends: reach out, encourage, share ...

Morning rituals: shower, dress, breakfast ...

Vitals: weight, blood pressure, etc.

Medical: medicines, treatments, etc.

Food & nutrition: morning, afternoon, evening (with calories) ...

Exercise: flexibility, cardio, resistance, sports ...

Evening rituals: dinner, family, bed ...

To dos:

Delegated, postponed, declined:

Accomplishments

What, where, when, how, why, who was I today ...

Month _____ Day ___ Year _____

Spiritual: pray, praise, serve ...

Family: love, listen, laugh ...

Friends: reach out, encourage, share ...

Morning rituals: shower, dress, breakfast ...

Vitals: weight, blood pressure, etc.

Medical: medicines, treatments, etc.

Food & nutrition: morning, afternoon, evening (with calories) ...

Exercise: flexibility, cardio, resistance, sports ...

Evening rituals: dinner, family, bed ...

To dos:

Delegated, postponed, declined:

Accomplishments

What, where, when, how, why, who was I today ...

Month _____ Day ___ Year _____

Spiritual: pray, praise, serve ...

Family: love, listen, laugh ...

Friends: reach out, encourage, share ...

Morning rituals: shower, dress, breakfast ...

Vitals: weight, blood pressure, etc.

Medical: medicines, treatments, etc.

Food & nutrition: morning, afternoon, evening (with calories) ...

Exercise: flexibility, cardio, resistance, sports ...

Evening rituals: dinner, family, bed ...

To dos:

Delegated, postponed, declined:

Accomplishments

What, where, when, how, why, who was I today ...

Spiritual: pray, praise, serve ...

Family: love, listen, laugh ...

Friends: reach out, encourage, share ...

Morning rituals: shower, dress, breakfast ...

Vitals: weight, blood pressure, etc.

Medical: medicines, treatments, etc.

Food & nutrition: morning, afternoon, evening (with calories) ...

Exercise: flexibility, cardio, resistance, sports ...

Evening rituals: dinner, family, bed ...

To dos:

Delegated, postponed, declined:

Accomplishments

What, where, when, how, why, who was I today ...

Month _____ Day ___ Year _____

Spiritual: pray, praise, serve ...

Family: love, listen, laugh ...

Friends: reach out, encourage, share ...

Morning rituals: shower, dress, breakfast ...

Vitals: weight, blood pressure, etc.

Medical: medicines, treatments, etc.

Food & nutrition: morning, afternoon, evening (with calories) ...

Exercise: flexibility, cardio, resistance, sports ...

Evening rituals: dinner, family, bed ...

To dos:

Delegated, postponed, declined:

Accomplishments

What, where, when, how, why, who was I today ...

Month _____ Day ___ Year _____

Spiritual: pray, praise, serve ...

Family: love, listen, laugh ...

Friends: reach out, encourage, share ...

Morning rituals: shower, dress, breakfast ...

Vitals: weight, blood pressure, etc.

Medical: medicines, treatments, etc.

Food & nutrition: morning, afternoon, evening (with calories) ...

Exercise: flexibility, cardio, resistance, sports ...

Evening rituals: dinner, family, bed ...

To dos:

Delegated, postponed, declined:

Accomplishments

What, where, when, how, why, who was I today ...

Month _____ Day ___ Year _____

Spiritual: pray, praise, serve ...

Family: love, listen, laugh ...

Friends: reach out, encourage, share ...

Morning rituals: shower, dress, breakfast ...

Vitals: weight, blood pressure, etc.

Medical: medicines, treatments, etc.

Food & nutrition: morning, afternoon, evening (with calories) ...

Exercise: flexibility, cardio, resistance, sports ...

Evening rituals: dinner, family, bed ...

To dos:

Delegated, postponed, declined:

Accomplishments

What, where, when, how, why, who was I today ...

Month _____ Day ___ Year _____

Spiritual: pray, praise, serve ...

Family: love, listen, laugh ...

Friends: reach out, encourage, share ...

Morning rituals: shower, dress, breakfast ...

Vitals: weight, blood pressure, etc.

Medical: medicines, treatments, etc.

Food & nutrition: morning, afternoon, evening (with calories) ...

Exercise: flexibility, cardio, resistance, sports ...

Evening rituals: dinner, family, bed ...

To dos:

Delegated, postponed, declined:

Accomplishments

What, where, when, how, why, who was I today ...

Month _____ Day ___ Year _____

Spiritual: pray, praise, serve ...

Family: love, listen, laugh ...

Friends: reach out, encourage, share ...

Morning rituals: shower, dress, breakfast ...

Vitals: weight, blood pressure, etc.

Medical: medicines, treatments, etc.

Food & nutrition: morning, afternoon, evening (with calories) ...

Exercise: flexibility, cardio, resistance, sports ...

Evening rituals: dinner, family, bed ...

To dos:

Delegated, postponed, declined:

Accomplishments

What, where, when, how, why, who was I today ...

Spiritual: pray, praise, serve ...

Family: love, listen, laugh ...

Friends: reach out, encourage, share ...

Morning rituals: shower, dress, breakfast ...

Vitals: weight, blood pressure, etc.

Medical: medicines, treatments, etc.

Food & nutrition: morning, afternoon, evening (with calories) ...

Exercise: flexibility, cardio, resistance, sports ...

Evening rituals: dinner, family, bed ...

To dos:

Delegated, postponed, declined:

Accomplishments

What, where, when, how, why, who was I today ...

Month _____ Day ___ Year _____

Spiritual: pray, praise, serve ...

Family: love, listen, laugh ...

Friends: reach out, encourage, share ...

Morning rituals: shower, dress, breakfast ...

Vitals: weight, blood pressure, etc.

Medical: medicines, treatments, etc.

Food & nutrition: morning, afternoon, evening (with calories) ...

Exercise: flexibility, cardio, resistance, sports ...

Evening rituals: dinner, family, bed ...

To dos:

Delegated, postponed, declined:

Accomplishments

What, where, when, how, why, who was I today ...

Month _____ Day ___ Year _____

Spiritual: pray, praise, serve ...

Family: love, listen, laugh ...

Friends: reach out, encourage, share ...

Morning rituals: shower, dress, breakfast ...

Vitals: weight, blood pressure, etc.

Medical: medicines, treatments, etc.

Food & nutrition: morning, afternoon, evening (with calories) ...

Exercise: flexibility, cardio, resistance, sports ...

Evening rituals: dinner, family, bed ...

To dos:

Delegated, postponed, declined:

Accomplishments

What, where, when, how, why, who was I today ...

Month _____ Day ___ Year _____

Spiritual: pray, praise, serve ...

Family: love, listen, laugh ...

Friends: reach out, encourage, share ...

Morning rituals: shower, dress, breakfast ...

Vitals: weight, blood pressure, etc.

Medical: medicines, treatments, etc.

Food & nutrition: morning, afternoon, evening (with calories) ...

Exercise: flexibility, cardio, resistance, sports ...

Evening rituals: dinner, family, bed ...

To dos:

Delegated, postponed, declined:

Accomplishments

What, where, when, how, why, who was I today ...

Spiritual: pray, praise, serve ...

Family: love, listen, laugh ...

Friends: reach out, encourage, share ...

Morning rituals: shower, dress, breakfast ...

Vitals: weight, blood pressure, etc.

Medical: medicines, treatments, etc.

Food & nutrition: morning, afternoon, evening (with calories) ...

Exercise: flexibility, cardio, resistance, sports ...

Evening rituals: dinner, family, bed ...

To dos:

Delegated, postponed, declined:

Accomplishments

What, where, when, how, why, who was I today ...

Month _____ Day ___ Year _____

Spiritual: pray, praise, serve ...

Family: love, listen, laugh ...

Friends: reach out, encourage, share ...

Morning rituals: shower, dress, breakfast ...

Vitals: weight, blood pressure, etc.

Medical: medicines, treatments, etc.

Food & nutrition: morning, afternoon, evening (with calories) ...

Exercise: flexibility, cardio, resistance, sports ...

Evening rituals: dinner, family, bed ...

To dos:

Delegated, postponed, declined:

Accomplishments

What, where, when, how, why, who was I today ...

Month _____ Day ___ Year _____

Spiritual: pray, praise, serve ...

Family: love, listen, laugh ...

Friends: reach out, encourage, share ...

Morning rituals: shower, dress, breakfast ...

Vitals: weight, blood pressure, etc.

Medical: medicines, treatments, etc.

Food & nutrition: morning, afternoon, evening (with calories) ...

Exercise: flexibility, cardio, resistance, sports ...

Evening rituals: dinner, family, bed ...

To dos:

Delegated, postponed, declined:

Accomplishments

What, where, when, how, why, who was I today ...

Month _____ Day ____ Year _____

Spiritual: pray, praise, serve ...

Family: love, listen, laugh ...

Friends: reach out, encourage, share ...

Morning rituals: shower, dress, breakfast ...

Vitals: weight, blood pressure, etc.

Medical: medicines, treatments, etc.

Food & nutrition: morning, afternoon, evening (with calories) ...

Exercise: flexibility, cardio, resistance, sports ...

Evening rituals: dinner, family, bed ...

To dos:

Delegated, postponed, declined:

Accomplishments

What, where, when, how, why, who was I today ...

Month _____ Day ___ Year _____

Spiritual: pray, praise, serve ...

Family: love, listen, laugh ...

Friends: reach out, encourage, share ...

Morning rituals: shower, dress, breakfast ...

Vitals: weight, blood pressure, etc.

Medical: medicines, treatments, etc.

Food & nutrition: morning, afternoon, evening (with calories) ...

Exercise: flexibility, cardio, resistance, sports ...

Evening rituals: dinner, family, bed ...

To dos:

Delegated, postponed, declined:

Accomplishments

What, where, when, how, why, who was I today ...

Month _____ Day ___ Year ____

Spiritual: pray, praise, serve ...

Family: love, listen, laugh ...

Friends: reach out, encourage, share ...

Morning rituals: shower, dress, breakfast ...

Vitals: weight, blood pressure, etc.

Medical: medicines, treatments, etc.

Food & nutrition: morning, afternoon, evening (with calories) ...

Exercise: flexibility, cardio, resistance, sports ...

Evening rituals: dinner, family, bed ...

To dos:

Delegated, postponed, declined:

Accomplishments

What, where, when, how, why, who was I today ...

Spiritual: pray, praise, serve ...

Family: love, listen, laugh ...

Friends: reach out, encourage, share ...

Morning rituals: shower, dress, breakfast ...

Vitals: weight, blood pressure, etc.

Medical: medicines, treatments, etc.

Food & nutrition: morning, afternoon, evening (with calories) ...

Exercise: flexibility, cardio, resistance, sports ...

Evening rituals: dinner, family, bed ...

To dos:

Delegated, postponed, declined:

Accomplishments

What, where, when, how, why, who was I today ...

Month _____ Day ___ Year _____

Spiritual: pray, praise, serve ...

Family: love, listen, laugh ...

Friends: reach out, encourage, share ...

Morning rituals: shower, dress, breakfast ...

Vitals: weight, blood pressure, etc.

Medical: medicines, treatments, etc.

Food & nutrition: morning, afternoon, evening (with calories) ...

Exercise: flexibility, cardio, resistance, sports ...

Evening rituals: dinner, family, bed ...

To dos:

Delegated, postponed, declined:

Accomplishments

What, where, when, how, why, who was I today ...

Month _____ Day ___ Year _____

Spiritual: pray, praise, serve ...

Family: love, listen, laugh ...

Friends: reach out, encourage, share ...

Morning rituals: shower, dress, breakfast ...

Vitals: weight, blood pressure, etc.

Medical: medicines, treatments, etc.

Food & nutrition: morning, afternoon, evening (with calories) ...

Exercise: flexibility, cardio, resistance, sports ...

Evening rituals: dinner, family, bed ...

To dos:

Delegated, postponed, declined:

Accomplishments

What, where, when, how, why, who was I today ...

Month _____ Day ___ Year _____

Spiritual: pray, praise, serve ...

Family: love, listen, laugh ...

Friends: reach out, encourage, share ...

Morning rituals: shower, dress, breakfast ...

Vitals: weight, blood pressure, etc.

Medical: medicines, treatments, etc.

Food & nutrition: morning, afternoon, evening (with calories) ...

Exercise: flexibility, cardio, resistance, sports ...

Evening rituals: dinner, family, bed ...

To dos:

Delegated, postponed, declined:

Accomplishments

What, where, when, how, why, who was I today ...

Month _____ Day ___ Year _____

Spiritual: pray, praise, serve ...

Family: love, listen, laugh ...

Friends: reach out, encourage, share ...

Morning rituals: shower, dress, breakfast ...

Vitals: weight, blood pressure, etc.

Medical: medicines, treatments, etc.

Food & nutrition: morning, afternoon, evening (with calories) ...

Exercise: flexibility, cardio, resistance, sports ...

Evening rituals: dinner, family, bed ...

To dos:

Delegated, postponed, declined:

Accomplishments

What, where, when, how, why, who was I today ...

Month _____ Day ___ Year _____

Spiritual: pray, praise, serve ...

Family: love, listen, laugh ...

Friends: reach out, encourage, share ...

Morning rituals: shower, dress, breakfast ...

Vitals: weight, blood pressure, etc.

Medical: medicines, treatments, etc.

Food & nutrition: morning, afternoon, evening (with calories) ...

Exercise: flexibility, cardio, resistance, sports ...

Evening rituals: dinner, family, bed ...

To dos:

Delegated, postponed, declined:

Accomplishments

What, where, when, how, why, who was I today ...

Month _____ Day ___ Year _____

Spiritual: pray, praise, serve ...

Family: love, listen, laugh ...

Friends: reach out, encourage, share ...

Morning rituals: shower, dress, breakfast ...

Vitals: weight, blood pressure, etc.

Medical: medicines, treatments, etc.

Food & nutrition: morning, afternoon, evening (with calories) ...

Exercise: flexibility, cardio, resistance, sports ...

Evening rituals: dinner, family, bed ...

To dos:

Delegated, postponed, declined:

Accomplishments

What, where, when, how, why, who was I today ...

Month _____ Day ___ Year _____

Spiritual: pray, praise, serve ...

Family: love, listen, laugh ...

Friends: reach out, encourage, share ...

Morning rituals: shower, dress, breakfast ...

Vitals: weight, blood pressure, etc.

Medical: medicines, treatments, etc.

Food & nutrition: morning, afternoon, evening (with calories) ...

Exercise: flexibility, cardio, resistance, sports ...

Evening rituals: dinner, family, bed ...

To dos:

Delegated, postponed, declined:

Accomplishments

What, where, when, how, why, who was I today ...

Month _____ Day ___ Year _____

Spiritual: pray, praise, serve ...

Family: love, listen, laugh ...

Friends: reach out, encourage, share ...

Morning rituals: shower, dress, breakfast ...

Vitals: weight, blood pressure, etc.

Medical: medicines, treatments, etc.

Food & nutrition: morning, afternoon, evening (with calories) ...

Exercise: flexibility, cardio, resistance, sports ...

Evening rituals: dinner, family, bed ...

To dos:

Delegated, postponed, declined:

Accomplishments

What, where, when, how, why, who was I today ...

Month _____ Day ___ Year _____

Spiritual: pray, praise, serve ...

Family: love, listen, laugh ...

Friends: reach out, encourage, share ...

Morning rituals: shower, dress, breakfast ...

Vitals: weight, blood pressure, etc.

Medical: medicines, treatments, etc.

Food & nutrition: morning, afternoon, evening (with calories) ...

Exercise: flexibility, cardio, resistance, sports ...

Evening rituals: dinner, family, bed ...

To dos:

Delegated, postponed, declined:

Accomplishments

What, where, when, how, why, who was I today ...

Month _____ Day ___ Year _____

Spiritual: pray, praise, serve ...

Family: love, listen, laugh ...

Friends: reach out, encourage, share ...

Morning rituals: shower, dress, breakfast ...

Vitals: weight, blood pressure, etc.

Medical: medicines, treatments, etc.

Food & nutrition: morning, afternoon, evening (with calories) ...

Exercise: flexibility, cardio, resistance, sports ...

Evening rituals: dinner, family, bed ...

To dos:

Delegated, postponed, declined:

Accomplishments

What, where, when, how, why, who was I today ...

Month _____ Day ___ Year _____

Spiritual: pray, praise, serve ...

Family: love, listen, laugh ...

Friends: reach out, encourage, share ...

Morning rituals: shower, dress, breakfast ...

Vitals: weight, blood pressure, etc.

Medical: medicines, treatments, etc.

Food & nutrition: morning, afternoon, evening (with calories) ...

Exercise: flexibility, cardio, resistance, sports ...

Evening rituals: dinner, family, bed ...

To dos:

Delegated, postponed, declined:

Accomplishments

What, where, when, how, why, who was I today ...

Month _____ Day ___ Year _____

Spiritual: pray, praise, serve ...

Family: love, listen, laugh ...

Friends: reach out, encourage, share ...

Morning rituals: shower, dress, breakfast ...

Vitals: weight, blood pressure, etc.

Medical: medicines, treatments, etc.

Food & nutrition: morning, afternoon, evening (with calories) ...

Exercise: flexibility, cardio, resistance, sports ...

Evening rituals: dinner, family, bed ...

To dos:

Delegated, postponed, declined:

Accomplishments

What, where, when, how, why, who was I today ...

Month _____ Day ___ Year _____

Spiritual: pray, praise, serve ...

Family: love, listen, laugh ...

Friends: reach out, encourage, share ...

Morning rituals: shower, dress, breakfast ...

Vitals: weight, blood pressure, etc.

Medical: medicines, treatments, etc.

Food & nutrition: morning, afternoon, evening (with calories) ...

Exercise: flexibility, cardio, resistance, sports ...

Evening rituals: dinner, family, bed ...

To dos:

Delegated, postponed, declined:

Accomplishments

What, where, when, how, why, who was I today ...

Spiritual: pray, praise, serve ...

Family: love, listen, laugh ...

Friends: reach out, encourage, share ...

Morning rituals: shower, dress, breakfast ...

Vitals: weight, blood pressure, etc.

Medical: medicines, treatments, etc.

Food & nutrition: morning, afternoon, evening (with calories) ...

Exercise: flexibility, cardio, resistance, sports ...

Evening rituals: dinner, family, bed ...

To dos:

Delegated, postponed, declined:

Accomplishments

What, where, when, how, why, who was I today ...

Month _____ Day ___ Year _____

Spiritual: pray, praise, serve ...

Family: love, listen, laugh ...

Friends: reach out, encourage, share ...

Morning rituals: shower, dress, breakfast ...

Vitals: weight, blood pressure, etc.

Medical: medicines, treatments, etc.

Food & nutrition: morning, afternoon, evening (with calories) ...

Exercise: flexibility, cardio, resistance, sports ...

Evening rituals: dinner, family, bed ...

To dos:

Delegated, postponed, declined:

Accomplishments

What, where, when, how, why, who was I today ...

Spiritual: pray, praise, serve ...

Family: love, listen, laugh ...

Friends: reach out, encourage, share ...

Morning rituals: shower, dress, breakfast ...

Vitals: weight, blood pressure, etc.

Medical: medicines, treatments, etc.

Food & nutrition: morning, afternoon, evening (with calories) ...

Exercise: flexibility, cardio, resistance, sports ...

Evening rituals: dinner, family, bed ...

To dos:

Delegated, postponed, declined:

Accomplishments

What, where, when, how, why, who was I today ...

Month _____ Day ___ Year _____

Spiritual: pray, praise, serve ...

Family: love, listen, laugh ...

Friends: reach out, encourage, share ...

Morning rituals: shower, dress, breakfast ...

Vitals: weight, blood pressure, etc.

Medical: medicines, treatments, etc.

Food & nutrition: morning, afternoon, evening (with calories) ...

Exercise: flexibility, cardio, resistance, sports ...

Evening rituals: dinner, family, bed ...

To dos:

Delegated, postponed, declined:

Accomplishments

What, where, when, how, why, who was I today ...

Month _____ Day ___ Year _____

Spiritual: pray, praise, serve ...

Family: love, listen, laugh ...

Friends: reach out, encourage, share ...

Morning rituals: shower, dress, breakfast ...

Vitals: weight, blood pressure, etc.

Medical: medicines, treatments, etc.

Food & nutrition: morning, afternoon, evening (with calories) ...

Exercise: flexibility, cardio, resistance, sports ...

Evening rituals: dinner, family, bed ...

To dos:

Delegated, postponed, declined:

Accomplishments

What, where, when, how, why, who was I today ...

Month _____ Day ___ Year _____

Spiritual: pray, praise, serve ...

Family: love, listen, laugh ...

Friends: reach out, encourage, share ...

Morning rituals: shower, dress, breakfast ...

Vitals: weight, blood pressure, etc.

Medical: medicines, treatments, etc.

Food & nutrition: morning, afternoon, evening (with calories) ...

Exercise: flexibility, cardio, resistance, sports ...

Evening rituals: dinner, family, bed ...

To dos:

Delegated, postponed, declined:

Accomplishments

What, where, when, how, why, who was I today ...

Month _____ Day ____ Year _____

Spiritual: pray, praise, serve ...

Family: love, listen, laugh ...

Friends: reach out, encourage, share ...

Morning rituals: shower, dress, breakfast ...

Vitals: weight, blood pressure, etc.

Medical: medicines, treatments, etc.

Food & nutrition: morning, afternoon, evening (with calories) ...

Exercise: flexibility, cardio, resistance, sports ...

Evening rituals: dinner, family, bed ...

To dos:

Delegated, postponed, declined:

Accomplishments

What, where, when, how, why, who was I today ...

Month _____ Day ___ Year _____

Spiritual: pray, praise, serve ...

Family: love, listen, laugh ...

Friends: reach out, encourage, share ...

Morning rituals: shower, dress, breakfast ...

Vitals: weight, blood pressure, etc.

Medical: medicines, treatments, etc.

Food & nutrition: morning, afternoon, evening (with calories) ...

Exercise: flexibility, cardio, resistance, sports ...

Evening rituals: dinner, family, bed ...

To dos:

Delegated, postponed, declined:

Accomplishments

What, where, when, how, why, who was I today ...

Month _____ Day ___ Year _____

Spiritual: pray, praise, serve ...

Family: love, listen, laugh ...

Friends: reach out, encourage, share ...

Morning rituals: shower, dress, breakfast ...

Vitals: weight, blood pressure, etc.

Medical: medicines, treatments, etc.

Food & nutrition: morning, afternoon, evening (with calories) ...

Exercise: flexibility, cardio, resistance, sports ...

Evening rituals: dinner, family, bed ...

To dos:

Delegated, postponed, declined:

Accomplishments

What, where, when, how, why, who was I today ...

Month _____ Day ___ Year _____

Spiritual: pray, praise, serve ...

Family: love, listen, laugh ...

Friends: reach out, encourage, share ...

Morning rituals: shower, dress, breakfast ...

Vitals: weight, blood pressure, etc.

Medical: medicines, treatments, etc.

Food & nutrition: morning, afternoon, evening (with calories) ...

Exercise: flexibility, cardio, resistance, sports ...

Evening rituals: dinner, family, bed ...

To dos:

Delegated, postponed, declined:

Accomplishments

What, where, when, how, why, who was I today ...

Month _____ Day ___ Year _____

Spiritual: pray, praise, serve ...

Family: love, listen, laugh ...

Friends: reach out, encourage, share ...

Morning rituals: shower, dress, breakfast ...

Vitals: weight, blood pressure, etc.

Medical: medicines, treatments, etc.

Food & nutrition: morning, afternoon, evening (with calories) ...

Exercise: flexibility, cardio, resistance, sports ...

Evening rituals: dinner, family, bed ...

To dos:

Delegated, postponed, declined:

Accomplishments

What, where, when, how, why, who was I today ...

Month _____ Day ___ Year _____

Spiritual: pray, praise, serve ...

Family: love, listen, laugh ...

Friends: reach out, encourage, share ...

Morning rituals: shower, dress, breakfast ...

Vitals: weight, blood pressure, etc.

Medical: medicines, treatments, etc.

Food & nutrition: morning, afternoon, evening (with calories) ...

Exercise: flexibility, cardio, resistance, sports ...

Evening rituals: dinner, family, bed ...

To dos:

Delegated, postponed, declined:

Accomplishments

What, where, when, how, why, who was I today ...

Month _____ Day ___ Year _____

Spiritual: pray, praise, serve ...

Family: love, listen, laugh ...

Friends: reach out, encourage, share ...

Morning rituals: shower, dress, breakfast ...

Vitals: weight, blood pressure, etc.

Medical: medicines, treatments, etc.

Food & nutrition: morning, afternoon, evening (with calories) ...

Exercise: flexibility, cardio, resistance, sports ...

Evening rituals: dinner, family, bed ...

To dos:

Delegated, postponed, declined:

Accomplishments

What, where, when, how, why, who was I today ...

Month _____ Day ___ Year _____

Spiritual: pray, praise, serve ...

Family: love, listen, laugh ...

Friends: reach out, encourage, share ...

Morning rituals: shower, dress, breakfast ...

Vitals: weight, blood pressure, etc.

Medical: medicines, treatments, etc.

Food & nutrition: morning, afternoon, evening (with calories) ...

Exercise: flexibility, cardio, resistance, sports ...

Evening rituals: dinner, family, bed ...

To dos:

Delegated, postponed, declined:

Accomplishments

What, where, when, how, why, who was I today ...

Month _____ Day ___ Year _____

Spiritual: pray, praise, serve ...

Family: love, listen, laugh ...

Friends: reach out, encourage, share ...

Morning rituals: shower, dress, breakfast ...

Vitals: weight, blood pressure, etc.

Medical: medicines, treatments, etc.

Food & nutrition: morning, afternoon, evening (with calories) ...

Exercise: flexibility, cardio, resistance, sports ...

Evening rituals: dinner, family, bed ...

To dos:

Delegated, postponed, declined:

Accomplishments

What, where, when, how, why, who was I today ...

Month _____ Day ___ Year _____

Spiritual: pray, praise, serve ...

Family: love, listen, laugh ...

Friends: reach out, encourage, share ...

Morning rituals: shower, dress, breakfast ...

Vitals: weight, blood pressure, etc.

Medical: medicines, treatments, etc.

Food & nutrition: morning, afternoon, evening (with calories) ...

Exercise: flexibility, cardio, resistance, sports ...

Evening rituals: dinner, family, bed ...

To dos:

Delegated, postponed, declined:

Accomplishments

What, where, when, how, why, who was I today ...

Spiritual: pray, praise, serve ...

Family: love, listen, laugh ...

Friends: reach out, encourage, share ...

Morning rituals: shower, dress, breakfast ...

Vitals: weight, blood pressure, etc.

Medical: medicines, treatments, etc.

Food & nutrition: morning, afternoon, evening (with calories) ...

Exercise: flexibility, cardio, resistance, sports ...

Evening rituals: dinner, family, bed ...

To dos:

Delegated, postponed, declined:

Accomplishments

What, where, when, how, why, who was I today ...

Month _____ Day ___ Year _____

Spiritual: pray, praise, serve ...

Family: love, listen, laugh ...

Friends: reach out, encourage, share ...

Morning rituals: shower, dress, breakfast ...

Vitals: weight, blood pressure, etc.

Medical: medicines, treatments, etc.

Food & nutrition: morning, afternoon, evening (with calories) ...

Exercise: flexibility, cardio, resistance, sports ...

Evening rituals: dinner, family, bed ...

To dos:

Delegated, postponed, declined:

Accomplishments

What, where, when, how, why, who was I today ...

Spiritual: pray, praise, serve ...

Family: love, listen, laugh ...

Friends: reach out, encourage, share ...

Morning rituals: shower, dress, breakfast ...

Vitals: weight, blood pressure, etc.

Medical: medicines, treatments, etc.

Food & nutrition: morning, afternoon, evening (with calories) ...

Exercise: flexibility, cardio, resistance, sports ...

Evening rituals: dinner, family, bed ...

To dos:

Delegated, postponed, declined:

Accomplishments

What, where, when, how, why, who was I today ...

Month _____ Day ___ Year _____

Spiritual: pray, praise, serve ...

Family: love, listen, laugh ...

Friends: reach out, encourage, share ...

Morning rituals: shower, dress, breakfast ...

Vitals: weight, blood pressure, etc.

Medical: medicines, treatments, etc.

Food & nutrition: morning, afternoon, evening (with calories) ...

Exercise: flexibility, cardio, resistance, sports ...

Evening rituals: dinner, family, bed ...

To dos:

Delegated, postponed, declined:

Accomplishments

What, where, when, how, why, who was I today ...

Month _____ Day ___ Year _____

Spiritual: pray, praise, serve ...

Family: love, listen, laugh ...

Friends: reach out, encourage, share ...

Morning rituals: shower, dress, breakfast ...

Vitals: weight, blood pressure, etc.

Medical: medicines, treatments, etc.

Food & nutrition: morning, afternoon, evening (with calories) ...

Exercise: flexibility, cardio, resistance, sports ...

Evening rituals: dinner, family, bed ...

To dos:

Delegated, postponed, declined:

Accomplishments

What, where, when, how, why, who was I today ...

Month _____ Day ___ Year _____

Spiritual: pray, praise, serve ...

Family: love, listen, laugh ...

Friends: reach out, encourage, share ...

Morning rituals: shower, dress, breakfast ...

Vitals: weight, blood pressure, etc.

Medical: medicines, treatments, etc.

Food & nutrition: morning, afternoon, evening (with calories) ...

Exercise: flexibility, cardio, resistance, sports ...

Evening rituals: dinner, family, bed ...

To dos:

Delegated, postponed, declined:

Accomplishments

What, where, when, how, why, who was I today ...

Month _____ Day ___ Year _____

Spiritual: pray, praise, serve ...

Family: love, listen, laugh ...

Friends: reach out, encourage, share ...

Morning rituals: shower, dress, breakfast ...

Vitals: weight, blood pressure, etc.

Medical: medicines, treatments, etc.

Food & nutrition: morning, afternoon, evening (with calories) ...

Exercise: flexibility, cardio, resistance, sports ...

Evening rituals: dinner, family, bed ...

To dos:

Delegated, postponed, declined:

Accomplishments

What, where, when, how, why, who was I today ...

Month _____ Day ___ Year _____

Spiritual: pray, praise, serve ...

Family: love, listen, laugh ...

Friends: reach out, encourage, share ...

Morning rituals: shower, dress, breakfast ...

Vitals: weight, blood pressure, etc.

Medical: medicines, treatments, etc.

Food & nutrition: morning, afternoon, evening (with calories) ...

Exercise: flexibility, cardio, resistance, sports ...

Evening rituals: dinner, family, bed ...

To dos:

Delegated, postponed, declined:

Accomplishments

What, where, when, how, why, who was I today ...

Month _____ Day ____ Year _____

Spiritual: pray, praise, serve ...

Family: love, listen, laugh ...

Friends: reach out, encourage, share ...

Morning rituals: shower, dress, breakfast ...

Vitals: weight, blood pressure, etc.

Medical: medicines, treatments, etc.

Food & nutrition: morning, afternoon, evening (with calories) ...

Exercise: flexibility, cardio, resistance, sports ...

Evening rituals: dinner, family, bed ...

To dos:

Delegated, postponed, declined:

Accomplishments

What, where, when, how, why, who was I today ...

Month _____ Day ___ Year _____

Spiritual: pray, praise, serve ...

Family: love, listen, laugh ...

Friends: reach out, encourage, share ...

Morning rituals: shower, dress, breakfast ...

Vitals: weight, blood pressure, etc.

Medical: medicines, treatments, etc.

Food & nutrition: morning, afternoon, evening (with calories) ...

Exercise: flexibility, cardio, resistance, sports ...

Evening rituals: dinner, family, bed ...

To dos:

Delegated, postponed, declined:

Accomplishments

What, where, when, how, why, who was I today ...

Month _____ Day ___ Year _____

Spiritual: pray, praise, serve ...

Family: love, listen, laugh ...

Friends: reach out, encourage, share ...

Morning rituals: shower, dress, breakfast ...

Vitals: weight, blood pressure, etc.

Medical: medicines, treatments, etc.

Food & nutrition: morning, afternoon, evening (with calories) ...

Exercise: flexibility, cardio, resistance, sports ...

Evening rituals: dinner, family, bed ...

To dos:

Delegated, postponed, declined:

Accomplishments

What, where, when, how, why, who was I today ...

Month _____ Day ___ Year _____

Spiritual: pray, praise, serve ...

Family: love, listen, laugh ...

Friends: reach out, encourage, share ...

Morning rituals: shower, dress, breakfast ...

Vitals: weight, blood pressure, etc.

Medical: medicines, treatments, etc.

Food & nutrition: morning, afternoon, evening (with calories) ...

Exercise: flexibility, cardio, resistance, sports ...

Evening rituals: dinner, family, bed ...

To dos:

Delegated, postponed, declined:

Accomplishments

What, where, when, how, why, who was I today ...

Month _____ Day ___ Year _____

Spiritual: pray, praise, serve ...

Family: love, listen, laugh ...

Friends: reach out, encourage, share ...

Morning rituals: shower, dress, breakfast ...

Vitals: weight, blood pressure, etc.

Medical: medicines, treatments, etc.

Food & nutrition: morning, afternoon, evening (with calories) ...

Exercise: flexibility, cardio, resistance, sports ...

Evening rituals: dinner, family, bed ...

To dos:

Delegated, postponed, declined:

Accomplishments

What, where, when, how, why, who was I today ...

Month _____ Day ___ Year _____

Spiritual: pray, praise, serve ...

Family: love, listen, laugh ...

Friends: reach out, encourage, share ...

Morning rituals: shower, dress, breakfast ...

Vitals: weight, blood pressure, etc.

Medical: medicines, treatments, etc.

Food & nutrition: morning, afternoon, evening (with calories) ...

Exercise: flexibility, cardio, resistance, sports ...

Evening rituals: dinner, family, bed ...

To dos:

Delegated, postponed, declined:

Accomplishments

What, where, when, how, why, who was I today ...

Month _____ Day ___ Year _____

Spiritual: pray, praise, serve ...

Family: love, listen, laugh ...

Friends: reach out, encourage, share ...

Morning rituals: shower, dress, breakfast ...

Vitals: weight, blood pressure, etc.

Medical: medicines, treatments, etc.

Food & nutrition: morning, afternoon, evening (with calories) ...

Exercise: flexibility, cardio, resistance, sports ...

Evening rituals: dinner, family, bed ...

To dos:

Delegated, postponed, declined:

Accomplishments

What, where, when, how, why, who was I today ...

Month _____ Day ___ Year _____

Spiritual: pray, praise, serve ...

Family: love, listen, laugh ...

Friends: reach out, encourage, share ...

Morning rituals: shower, dress, breakfast ...

Vitals: weight, blood pressure, etc.

Medical: medicines, treatments, etc.

Food & nutrition: morning, afternoon, evening (with calories) ...

Exercise: flexibility, cardio, resistance, sports ...

Evening rituals: dinner, family, bed ...

To dos:

Delegated, postponed, declined:

Accomplishments

What, where, when, how, why, who was I today ...

Month _____ Day ___ Year _____

Spiritual: pray, praise, serve ...

Family: love, listen, laugh ...

Friends: reach out, encourage, share ...

Morning rituals: shower, dress, breakfast ...

Vitals: weight, blood pressure, etc.

Medical: medicines, treatments, etc.

Food & nutrition: morning, afternoon, evening (with calories) ...

Exercise: flexibility, cardio, resistance, sports ...

Evening rituals: dinner, family, bed ...

To dos:

Delegated, postponed, declined:

Accomplishments

What, where, when, how, why, who was I today ...

Month _____ Day ___ Year _____

Spiritual: pray, praise, serve ...

Family: love, listen, laugh ...

Friends: reach out, encourage, share ...

Morning rituals: shower, dress, breakfast ...

Vitals: weight, blood pressure, etc.

Medical: medicines, treatments, etc.

Food & nutrition: morning, afternoon, evening (with calories) ...

Exercise: flexibility, cardio, resistance, sports ...

Evening rituals: dinner, family, bed ...

To dos:

Delegated, postponed, declined:

Accomplishments

What, where, when, how, why, who was I today ...

Month _____ Day ___ Year _____

Spiritual: pray, praise, serve ...

Family: love, listen, laugh ...

Friends: reach out, encourage, share ...

Morning rituals: shower, dress, breakfast ...

Vitals: weight, blood pressure, etc.

Medical: medicines, treatments, etc.

Food & nutrition: morning, afternoon, evening (with calories) ...

Exercise: flexibility, cardio, resistance, sports ...

Evening rituals: dinner, family, bed ...

To dos:

Delegated, postponed, declined:

Accomplishments

What, where, when, how, why, who was I today ...

Month _____ Day ___ Year _____

Spiritual: pray, praise, serve ...

Family: love, listen, laugh ...

Friends: reach out, encourage, share ...

Morning rituals: shower, dress, breakfast ...

Vitals: weight, blood pressure, etc.

Medical: medicines, treatments, etc.

Food & nutrition: morning, afternoon, evening (with calories) ...

Exercise: flexibility, cardio, resistance, sports ...

Evening rituals: dinner, family, bed ...

To dos:

Delegated, postponed, declined:

Accomplishments

What, where, when, how, why, who was I today ...

Month _____ Day ___ Year _____

Spiritual: pray, praise, serve ...

Family: love, listen, laugh ...

Friends: reach out, encourage, share ...

Morning rituals: shower, dress, breakfast ...

Vitals: weight, blood pressure, etc.

Medical: medicines, treatments, etc.

Food & nutrition: morning, afternoon, evening (with calories) ...

Exercise: flexibility, cardio, resistance, sports ...

Evening rituals: dinner, family, bed ...

To dos:

Delegated, postponed, declined:

Accomplishments

What, where, when, how, why, who was I today ...

Month _____ Day ___ Year _____

Spiritual: pray, praise, serve ...

Family: love, listen, laugh ...

Friends: reach out, encourage, share ...

Morning rituals: shower, dress, breakfast ...

Vitals: weight, blood pressure, etc.

Medical: medicines, treatments, etc.

Food & nutrition: morning, afternoon, evening (with calories) ...

Exercise: flexibility, cardio, resistance, sports ...

Evening rituals: dinner, family, bed ...

To dos:

Delegated, postponed, declined:

Accomplishments

What, where, when, how, why, who was I today ...

Month _____ Day ___ Year _____

Spiritual: pray, praise, serve ...

Family: love, listen, laugh ...

Friends: reach out, encourage, share ...

Morning rituals: shower, dress, breakfast ...

Vitals: weight, blood pressure, etc.

Medical: medicines, treatments, etc.

Food & nutrition: morning, afternoon, evening (with calories) ...

Exercise: flexibility, cardio, resistance, sports ...

Evening rituals: dinner, family, bed ...

To dos:

Delegated, postponed, declined:

Accomplishments

What, where, when, how, why, who was I today ...

Month _____ Day ___ Year _____

Spiritual: pray, praise, serve ...

Family: love, listen, laugh ...

Friends: reach out, encourage, share ...

Morning rituals: shower, dress, breakfast ...

Vitals: weight, blood pressure, etc.

Medical: medicines, treatments, etc.

Food & nutrition: morning, afternoon, evening (with calories) ...

Exercise: flexibility, cardio, resistance, sports ...

Evening rituals: dinner, family, bed ...

To dos:

Delegated, postponed, declined:

Accomplishments

What, where, when, how, why, who was I today ...

Month _____ Day ___ Year _____

Spiritual: pray, praise, serve ...

Family: love, listen, laugh ...

Friends: reach out, encourage, share ...

Morning rituals: shower, dress, breakfast ...

Vitals: weight, blood pressure, etc.

Medical: medicines, treatments, etc.

Food & nutrition: morning, afternoon, evening (with calories) ...

Exercise: flexibility, cardio, resistance, sports ...

Evening rituals: dinner, family, bed ...

To dos:

Delegated, postponed, declined:

Accomplishments

What, where, when, how, why, who was I today ...

Month _____ Day ___ Year _____

Spiritual: pray, praise, serve ...

Family: love, listen, laugh ...

Friends: reach out, encourage, share ...

Morning rituals: shower, dress, breakfast ...

Vitals: weight, blood pressure, etc.

Medical: medicines, treatments, etc.

Food & nutrition: morning, afternoon, evening (with calories) ...

Exercise: flexibility, cardio, resistance, sports ...

Evening rituals: dinner, family, bed ...

To dos:

Delegated, postponed, declined:

Accomplishments

What, where, when, how, why, who was I today ...

Spiritual: pray, praise, serve ...

Family: love, listen, laugh ...

Friends: reach out, encourage, share ...

Morning rituals: shower, dress, breakfast ...

Vitals: weight, blood pressure, etc.

Medical: medicines, treatments, etc.

Food & nutrition: morning, afternoon, evening (with calories) ...

Exercise: flexibility, cardio, resistance, sports ...

Evening rituals: dinner, family, bed ...

To dos:

Delegated, postponed, declined:

Accomplishments

What, where, when, how, why, who was I today ...

Month _____ Day ___ Year _____

Spiritual: pray, praise, serve ...

Family: love, listen, laugh ...

Friends: reach out, encourage, share ...

Morning rituals: shower, dress, breakfast ...

Vitals: weight, blood pressure, etc.

Medical: medicines, treatments, etc.

Food & nutrition: morning, afternoon, evening (with calories) ...

Exercise: flexibility, cardio, resistance, sports ...

Evening rituals: dinner, family, bed ...

To dos:

Delegated, postponed, declined:

Accomplishments

What, where, when, how, why, who was I today ...

Month _____ Day ___ Year _____

Spiritual: pray, praise, serve ...

Family: love, listen, laugh ...

Friends: reach out, encourage, share ...

Morning rituals: shower, dress, breakfast ...

Vitals: weight, blood pressure, etc.

Medical: medicines, treatments, etc.

Food & nutrition: morning, afternoon, evening (with calories) ...

Exercise: flexibility, cardio, resistance, sports ...

Evening rituals: dinner, family, bed ...

To dos:

Delegated, postponed, declined:

Accomplishments

What, where, when, how, why, who was I today ...

Month _____ Day ___ Year _____

Spiritual: pray, praise, serve ...

Family: love, listen, laugh ...

Friends: reach out, encourage, share ...

Morning rituals: shower, dress, breakfast ...

Vitals: weight, blood pressure, etc.

Medical: medicines, treatments, etc.

Food & nutrition: morning, afternoon, evening (with calories) ...

Exercise: flexibility, cardio, resistance, sports ...

Evening rituals: dinner, family, bed ...

To dos:

Delegated, postponed, declined:

Accomplishments

What, where, when, how, why, who was I today ...

Spiritual: pray, praise, serve ...

Family: love, listen, laugh ...

Friends: reach out, encourage, share ...

Morning rituals: shower, dress, breakfast ...

Vitals: weight, blood pressure, etc.

Medical: medicines, treatments, etc.

Food & nutrition: morning, afternoon, evening (with calories) ...

Exercise: flexibility, cardio, resistance, sports ...

Evening rituals: dinner, family, bed ...

To dos:

Delegated, postponed, declined:

Accomplishments

What, where, when, how, why, who was I today ...

Month _____ Day ___ Year _____

Spiritual: pray, praise, serve ...

Family: love, listen, laugh ...

Friends: reach out, encourage, share ...

Morning rituals: shower, dress, breakfast ...

Vitals: weight, blood pressure, etc.

Medical: medicines, treatments, etc.

Food & nutrition: morning, afternoon, evening (with calories) ...

Exercise: flexibility, cardio, resistance, sports ...

Evening rituals: dinner, family, bed ...

To dos:

Delegated, postponed, declined:

Accomplishments

What, where, when, how, why, who was I today ...

Spiritual: pray, praise, serve ...

Family: love, listen, laugh ...

Friends: reach out, encourage, share ...

Morning rituals: shower, dress, breakfast ...

Vitals: weight, blood pressure, etc.

Medical: medicines, treatments, etc.

Food & nutrition: morning, afternoon, evening (with calories) ...

Exercise: flexibility, cardio, resistance, sports ...

Evening rituals: dinner, family, bed ...

To dos:

Delegated, postponed, declined:

Accomplishments

What, where, when, how, why, who was I today ...

Month _____ Day ___ Year _____

Spiritual: pray, praise, serve ...

Family: love, listen, laugh ...

Friends: reach out, encourage, share ...

Morning rituals: shower, dress, breakfast ...

Vitals: weight, blood pressure, etc.

Medical: medicines, treatments, etc.

Food & nutrition: morning, afternoon, evening (with calories) ...

Exercise: flexibility, cardio, resistance, sports ...

Evening rituals: dinner, family, bed ...

To dos:

Delegated, postponed, declined:

Accomplishments

What, where, when, how, why, who was I today ...

Month _____ Day ___ Year _____

Spiritual: pray, praise, serve ...

Family: love, listen, laugh ...

Friends: reach out, encourage, share ...

Morning rituals: shower, dress, breakfast ...

Vitals: weight, blood pressure, etc.

Medical: medicines, treatments, etc.

Food & nutrition: morning, afternoon, evening (with calories) ...

Exercise: flexibility, cardio, resistance, sports ...

Evening rituals: dinner, family, bed ...

To dos:

Delegated, postponed, declined:

Accomplishments

What, where, when, how, why, who was I today ...

Month _____ Day ____ Year _____

Spiritual: pray, praise, serve ...

Family: love, listen, laugh ...

Friends: reach out, encourage, share ...

Morning rituals: shower, dress, breakfast ...

Vitals: weight, blood pressure, etc.

Medical: medicines, treatments, etc.

Food & nutrition: morning, afternoon, evening (with calories) ...

Exercise: flexibility, cardio, resistance, sports ...

Evening rituals: dinner, family, bed ...

To dos:

Delegated, postponed, declined:

Accomplishments

What, where, when, how, why, who was I today ...

Month _____ Day ___ Year _____

Spiritual: pray, praise, serve ...

Family: love, listen, laugh ...

Friends: reach out, encourage, share ...

Morning rituals: shower, dress, breakfast ...

Vitals: weight, blood pressure, etc.

Medical: medicines, treatments, etc.

Food & nutrition: morning, afternoon, evening (with calories) ...

Exercise: flexibility, cardio, resistance, sports ...

Evening rituals: dinner, family, bed ...

To dos:

Delegated, postponed, declined:

Accomplishments

What, where, when, how, why, who was I today ...

Month _____ Day ___ Year _____

Spiritual: pray, praise, serve ...

Family: love, listen, laugh ...

Friends: reach out, encourage, share ...

Morning rituals: shower, dress, breakfast ...

Vitals: weight, blood pressure, etc.

Medical: medicines, treatments, etc.

Food & nutrition: morning, afternoon, evening (with calories) ...

Exercise: flexibility, cardio, resistance, sports ...

Evening rituals: dinner, family, bed ...

To dos:

Delegated, postponed, declined:

Accomplishments

What, where, when, how, why, who was I today ...

Month _____ Day ___ Year _____

Spiritual: pray, praise, serve ...

Family: love, listen, laugh ...

Friends: reach out, encourage, share ...

Morning rituals: shower, dress, breakfast ...

Vitals: weight, blood pressure, etc.

Medical: medicines, treatments, etc.

Food & nutrition: morning, afternoon, evening (with calories) ...

Exercise: flexibility, cardio, resistance, sports ...

Evening rituals: dinner, family, bed ...

To dos:

Delegated, postponed, declined:

Accomplishments

What, where, when, how, why, who was I today ...

Month _____ Day ___ Year _____

Spiritual: pray, praise, serve ...

Family: love, listen, laugh ...

Friends: reach out, encourage, share ...

Morning rituals: shower, dress, breakfast ...

Vitals: weight, blood pressure, etc.

Medical: medicines, treatments, etc.

Food & nutrition: morning, afternoon, evening (with calories) ...

Exercise: flexibility, cardio, resistance, sports ...

Evening rituals: dinner, family, bed ...

To dos:

Delegated, postponed, declined:

Accomplishments

What, where, when, how, why, who was I today ...

Month _____ Day ___ Year _____

Spiritual: pray, praise, serve ...

Family: love, listen, laugh ...

Friends: reach out, encourage, share ...

Morning rituals: shower, dress, breakfast ...

Vitals: weight, blood pressure, etc.

Medical: medicines, treatments, etc.

Food & nutrition: morning, afternoon, evening (with calories) ...

Exercise: flexibility, cardio, resistance, sports ...

Evening rituals: dinner, family, bed ...

To dos:

Delegated, postponed, declined:

Accomplishments

What, where, when, how, why, who was I today ...

Month _____ Day ____ Year _____

Spiritual: pray, praise, serve ...

Family: love, listen, laugh ...

Friends: reach out, encourage, share ...

Morning rituals: shower, dress, breakfast ...

Vitals: weight, blood pressure, etc.

Medical: medicines, treatments, etc.

Food & nutrition: morning, afternoon, evening (with calories) ...

Exercise: flexibility, cardio, resistance, sports ...

Evening rituals: dinner, family, bed ...

To dos:

Delegated, postponed, declined:

Accomplishments

What, where, when, how, why, who was I today ...

Month _____ Day ___ Year _____

Spiritual: pray, praise, serve ...

Family: love, listen, laugh ...

Friends: reach out, encourage, share ...

Morning rituals: shower, dress, breakfast ...

Vitals: weight, blood pressure, etc.

Medical: medicines, treatments, etc.

Food & nutrition: morning, afternoon, evening (with calories) ...

Exercise: flexibility, cardio, resistance, sports ...

Evening rituals: dinner, family, bed ...

To dos:

Delegated, postponed, declined:

Accomplishments

What, where, when, how, why, who was I today ...

Month _____ Day ___ Year _____

Spiritual: pray, praise, serve ...

Family: love, listen, laugh ...

Friends: reach out, encourage, share ...

Morning rituals: shower, dress, breakfast ...

Vitals: weight, blood pressure, etc.

Medical: medicines, treatments, etc.

Food & nutrition: morning, afternoon, evening (with calories) ...

Exercise: flexibility, cardio, resistance, sports ...

Evening rituals: dinner, family, bed ...

To dos:

Delegated, postponed, declined:

Accomplishments

What, where, when, how, why, who was I today ...

Month _____ Day ___ Year _____

Spiritual: pray, praise, serve ...

Family: love, listen, laugh ...

Friends: reach out, encourage, share ...

Morning rituals: shower, dress, breakfast ...

Vitals: weight, blood pressure, etc.

Medical: medicines, treatments, etc.

Food & nutrition: morning, afternoon, evening (with calories) ...

Exercise: flexibility, cardio, resistance, sports ...

Evening rituals: dinner, family, bed ...

To dos:

Delegated, postponed, declined:

Accomplishments

What, where, when, how, why, who was I today ...

Month _____ Day ___ Year _____

Spiritual: pray, praise, serve ...

Family: love, listen, laugh ...

Friends: reach out, encourage, share ...

Morning rituals: shower, dress, breakfast ...

Vitals: weight, blood pressure, etc.

Medical: medicines, treatments, etc.

Food & nutrition: morning, afternoon, evening (with calories) ...

Exercise: flexibility, cardio, resistance, sports ...

Evening rituals: dinner, family, bed ...

To dos:

Delegated, postponed, declined:

Accomplishments

What, where, when, how, why, who was I today ...

Spiritual: pray, praise, serve ...

Family: love, listen, laugh ...

Friends: reach out, encourage, share ...

Morning rituals: shower, dress, breakfast ...

Vitals: weight, blood pressure, etc.

Medical: medicines, treatments, etc.

Food & nutrition: morning, afternoon, evening (with calories) ...

Exercise: flexibility, cardio, resistance, sports ...

Evening rituals: dinner, family, bed ...

To dos:

Delegated, postponed, declined:

Accomplishments

What, where, when, how, why, who was I today ...

Month _____ Day ___ Year _____

Spiritual: pray, praise, serve ...

Family: love, listen, laugh ...

Friends: reach out, encourage, share ...

Morning rituals: shower, dress, breakfast ...

Vitals: weight, blood pressure, etc.

Medical: medicines, treatments, etc.

Food & nutrition: morning, afternoon, evening (with calories) ...

Exercise: flexibility, cardio, resistance, sports ...

Evening rituals: dinner, family, bed ...

To dos:

Delegated, postponed, declined:

Accomplishments

What, where, when, how, why, who was I today ...

Month _____ Day ___ Year _____

Spiritual: pray, praise, serve ...

Family: love, listen, laugh ...

Friends: reach out, encourage, share ...

Morning rituals: shower, dress, breakfast ...

Vitals: weight, blood pressure, etc.

Medical: medicines, treatments, etc.

Food & nutrition: morning, afternoon, evening (with calories) ...

Exercise: flexibility, cardio, resistance, sports ...

Evening rituals: dinner, family, bed ...

To dos:

Delegated, postponed, declined:

Accomplishments

What, where, when, how, why, who was I today ...

Month _____ Day ___ Year _____

Spiritual: pray, praise, serve ...

Family: love, listen, laugh ...

Friends: reach out, encourage, share ...

Morning rituals: shower, dress, breakfast ...

Vitals: weight, blood pressure, etc.

Medical: medicines, treatments, etc.

Food & nutrition: morning, afternoon, evening (with calories) ...

Exercise: flexibility, cardio, resistance, sports ...

Evening rituals: dinner, family, bed ...

To dos:

Delegated, postponed, declined:

Accomplishments

What, where, when, how, why, who was I today ...

Month _____ Day ____ Year _____

Spiritual: pray, praise, serve ...

Family: love, listen, laugh ...

Friends: reach out, encourage, share ...

Morning rituals: shower, dress, breakfast ...

Vitals: weight, blood pressure, etc.

Medical: medicines, treatments, etc.

Food & nutrition: morning, afternoon, evening (with calories) ...

Exercise: flexibility, cardio, resistance, sports ...

Evening rituals: dinner, family, bed ...

To dos:

Delegated, postponed, declined:

Accomplishments

What, where, when, how, why, who was I today ...

Month _____ Day ___ Year _____

Spiritual: pray, praise, serve ...

Family: love, listen, laugh ...

Friends: reach out, encourage, share ...

Morning rituals: shower, dress, breakfast ...

Vitals: weight, blood pressure, etc.

Medical: medicines, treatments, etc.

Food & nutrition: morning, afternoon, evening (with calories) ...

Exercise: flexibility, cardio, resistance, sports ...

Evening rituals: dinner, family, bed ...

To dos:

Delegated, postponed, declined:

Accomplishments

What, where, when, how, why, who was I today ...

Month _____ Day ___ Year _____

Spiritual: pray, praise, serve ...

Family: love, listen, laugh ...

Friends: reach out, encourage, share ...

Morning rituals: shower, dress, breakfast ...

Vitals: weight, blood pressure, etc.

Medical: medicines, treatments, etc.

Food & nutrition: morning, afternoon, evening (with calories) ...

Exercise: flexibility, cardio, resistance, sports ...

Evening rituals: dinner, family, bed ...

To dos:

Delegated, postponed, declined:

Accomplishments

What, where, when, how, why, who was I today ...

Month _____ Day ___ Year _____

Spiritual: pray, praise, serve ...

Family: love, listen, laugh ...

Friends: reach out, encourage, share ...

Morning rituals: shower, dress, breakfast ...

Vitals: weight, blood pressure, etc.

Medical: medicines, treatments, etc.

Food & nutrition: morning, afternoon, evening (with calories) ...

Exercise: flexibility, cardio, resistance, sports ...

Evening rituals: dinner, family, bed ...

To dos:

Delegated, postponed, declined:

Accomplishments

What, where, when, how, why, who was I today ...

Month _____ Day ___ Year _____

Spiritual: pray, praise, serve ...

Family: love, listen, laugh ...

Friends: reach out, encourage, share ...

Morning rituals: shower, dress, breakfast ...

Vitals: weight, blood pressure, etc.

Medical: medicines, treatments, etc.

Food & nutrition: morning, afternoon, evening (with calories) ...

Exercise: flexibility, cardio, resistance, sports ...

Evening rituals: dinner, family, bed ...

To dos:

Delegated, postponed, declined:

Accomplishments

What, where, when, how, why, who was I today ...

Month _____ Day ___ Year _____

Spiritual: pray, praise, serve ...

Family: love, listen, laugh ...

Friends: reach out, encourage, share ...

Morning rituals: shower, dress, breakfast ...

Vitals: weight, blood pressure, etc.

Medical: medicines, treatments, etc.

Food & nutrition: morning, afternoon, evening (with calories) ...

Exercise: flexibility, cardio, resistance, sports ...

Evening rituals: dinner, family, bed ...

To dos:

Delegated, postponed, declined:

Accomplishments

What, where, when, how, why, who was I today ...

Month _____ Day ___ Year _____

Spiritual: pray, praise, serve ...

Family: love, listen, laugh ...

Friends: reach out, encourage, share ...

Morning rituals: shower, dress, breakfast ...

Vitals: weight, blood pressure, etc.

Medical: medicines, treatments, etc.

Food & nutrition: morning, afternoon, evening (with calories) ...

Exercise: flexibility, cardio, resistance, sports ...

Evening rituals: dinner, family, bed ...

To dos:

Delegated, postponed, declined:

Accomplishments

What, where, when, how, why, who was I today ...

Month _____ Day ___ Year _____

Spiritual: pray, praise, serve ...

Family: love, listen, laugh ...

Friends: reach out, encourage, share ...

Morning rituals: shower, dress, breakfast ...

Vitals: weight, blood pressure, etc.

Medical: medicines, treatments, etc.

Food & nutrition: morning, afternoon, evening (with calories) ...

Exercise: flexibility, cardio, resistance, sports ...

Evening rituals: dinner, family, bed ...

To dos:

Delegated, postponed, declined:

Accomplishments

What, where, when, how, why, who was I today ...

Month _____ Day ___ Year _____

Spiritual: pray, praise, serve ...

Family: love, listen, laugh ...

Friends: reach out, encourage, share ...

Morning rituals: shower, dress, breakfast ...

Vitals: weight, blood pressure, etc.

Medical: medicines, treatments, etc.

Food & nutrition: morning, afternoon, evening (with calories) ...

Exercise: flexibility, cardio, resistance, sports ...

Evening rituals: dinner, family, bed ...

To dos:

Delegated, postponed, declined:

Accomplishments

What, where, when, how, why, who was I today ...

Month _____ Day ___ Year _____

Spiritual: pray, praise, serve ...

Family: love, listen, laugh ...

Friends: reach out, encourage, share ...

Morning rituals: shower, dress, breakfast ...

Vitals: weight, blood pressure, etc.

Medical: medicines, treatments, etc.

Food & nutrition: morning, afternoon, evening (with calories) ...

Exercise: flexibility, cardio, resistance, sports ...

Evening rituals: dinner, family, bed ...

To dos:

Delegated, postponed, declined:

Accomplishments

What, where, when, how, why, who was I today ...

Month _____ Day ___ Year _____

Spiritual: pray, praise, serve ...

Family: love, listen, laugh ...

Friends: reach out, encourage, share ...

Morning rituals: shower, dress, breakfast ...

Vitals: weight, blood pressure, etc.

Medical: medicines, treatments, etc.

Food & nutrition: morning, afternoon, evening (with calories) ...

Exercise: flexibility, cardio, resistance, sports ...

Evening rituals: dinner, family, bed ...

To dos:

Delegated, postponed, declined:

Accomplishments

What, where, when, how, why, who was I today ...

Month _____ Day ___ Year _____

Spiritual: pray, praise, serve ...

Family: love, listen, laugh ...

Friends: reach out, encourage, share ...

Morning rituals: shower, dress, breakfast ...

Vitals: weight, blood pressure, etc.

Medical: medicines, treatments, etc.

Food & nutrition: morning, afternoon, evening (with calories) ...

Exercise: flexibility, cardio, resistance, sports ...

Evening rituals: dinner, family, bed ...

To dos:

Delegated, postponed, declined:

Accomplishments

What, where, when, how, why, who was I today ...

Month _____ Day ___ Year _____

Spiritual: pray, praise, serve ...

Family: love, listen, laugh ...

Friends: reach out, encourage, share ...

Morning rituals: shower, dress, breakfast ...

Vitals: weight, blood pressure, etc.

Medical: medicines, treatments, etc.

Food & nutrition: morning, afternoon, evening (with calories) ...

Exercise: flexibility, cardio, resistance, sports ...

Evening rituals: dinner, family, bed ...

To dos:

Delegated, postponed, declined:

Accomplishments

What, where, when, how, why, who was I today ...

Month _____ Day ___ Year _____

Spiritual: pray, praise, serve ...

Family: love, listen, laugh ...

Friends: reach out, encourage, share ...

Morning rituals: shower, dress, breakfast ...

Vitals: weight, blood pressure, etc.

Medical: medicines, treatments, etc.

Food & nutrition: morning, afternoon, evening (with calories) ...

Exercise: flexibility, cardio, resistance, sports ...

Evening rituals: dinner, family, bed ...

To dos:

Delegated, postponed, declined:

Accomplishments

What, where, when, how, why, who was I today ...

Month _____ Day ___ Year _____

Spiritual: pray, praise, serve ...

Family: love, listen, laugh ...

Friends: reach out, encourage, share ...

Morning rituals: shower, dress, breakfast ...

Vitals: weight, blood pressure, etc.

Medical: medicines, treatments, etc.

Food & nutrition: morning, afternoon, evening (with calories) ...

Exercise: flexibility, cardio, resistance, sports ...

Evening rituals: dinner, family, bed ...

To dos:

Delegated, postponed, declined:

Accomplishments

What, where, when, how, why, who was I today ...

Month _____ Day ___ Year _____

Spiritual: pray, praise, serve ...

Family: love, listen, laugh ...

Friends: reach out, encourage, share ...

Morning rituals: shower, dress, breakfast ...

Vitals: weight, blood pressure, etc.

Medical: medicines, treatments, etc.

Food & nutrition: morning, afternoon, evening (with calories) ...

Exercise: flexibility, cardio, resistance, sports ...

Evening rituals: dinner, family, bed ...

To dos:

Delegated, postponed, declined:

Accomplishments

What, where, when, how, why, who was I today ...

Month _____ Day ___ Year _____

Spiritual: pray, praise, serve ...

Family: love, listen, laugh ...

Friends: reach out, encourage, share ...

Morning rituals: shower, dress, breakfast ...

Vitals: weight, blood pressure, etc.

Medical: medicines, treatments, etc.

Food & nutrition: morning, afternoon, evening (with calories) ...

Exercise: flexibility, cardio, resistance, sports ...

Evening rituals: dinner, family, bed ...

To dos:

Delegated, postponed, declined:

Accomplishments

What, where, when, how, why, who was I today ...

Month _____ Day ___ Year _____

Spiritual: pray, praise, serve ...

Family: love, listen, laugh ...

Friends: reach out, encourage, share ...

Morning rituals: shower, dress, breakfast ...

Vitals: weight, blood pressure, etc.

Medical: medicines, treatments, etc.

Food & nutrition: morning, afternoon, evening (with calories) ...

Exercise: flexibility, cardio, resistance, sports ...

Evening rituals: dinner, family, bed ...

To dos:

Delegated, postponed, declined:

Accomplishments

What, where, when, how, why, who was I today ...

Spiritual: pray, praise, serve ...

Family: love, listen, laugh ...

Friends: reach out, encourage, share ...

Morning rituals: shower, dress, breakfast ...

Vitals: weight, blood pressure, etc.

Medical: medicines, treatments, etc.

Food & nutrition: morning, afternoon, evening (with calories) ...

Exercise: flexibility, cardio, resistance, sports ...

Evening rituals: dinner, family, bed ...

To dos:

Delegated, postponed, declined:

Accomplishments

What, where, when, how, why, who was I today ...

Month _____ Day ___ Year _____

Spiritual: pray, praise, serve ...

Family: love, listen, laugh ...

Friends: reach out, encourage, share ...

Morning rituals: shower, dress, breakfast ...

Vitals: weight, blood pressure, etc.

Medical: medicines, treatments, etc.

Food & nutrition: morning, afternoon, evening (with calories) ...

Exercise: flexibility, cardio, resistance, sports ...

Evening rituals: dinner, family, bed ...

To dos:

Delegated, postponed, declined:

Accomplishments

What, where, when, how, why, who was I today ...

Month _____ Day ___ Year _____

Spiritual: pray, praise, serve ...

Family: love, listen, laugh ...

Friends: reach out, encourage, share ...

Morning rituals: shower, dress, breakfast ...

Vitals: weight, blood pressure, etc.

Medical: medicines, treatments, etc.

Food & nutrition: morning, afternoon, evening (with calories) ...

Exercise: flexibility, cardio, resistance, sports ...

Evening rituals: dinner, family, bed ...

To dos:

Delegated, postponed, declined:

Accomplishments

What, where, when, how, why, who was I today ...

Month _____ Day ___ Year _____

Spiritual: pray, praise, serve ...

Family: love, listen, laugh ...

Friends: reach out, encourage, share ...

Morning rituals: shower, dress, breakfast ...

Vitals: weight, blood pressure, etc.

Medical: medicines, treatments, etc.

Food & nutrition: morning, afternoon, evening (with calories) ...

Exercise: flexibility, cardio, resistance, sports ...

Evening rituals: dinner, family, bed ...

To dos:

Delegated, postponed, declined:

Accomplishments

What, where, when, how, why, who was I today ...

Spiritual: pray, praise, serve ...

Family: love, listen, laugh ...

Friends: reach out, encourage, share ...

Morning rituals: shower, dress, breakfast ...

Vitals: weight, blood pressure, etc.

Medical: medicines, treatments, etc.

Food & nutrition: morning, afternoon, evening (with calories) ...

Exercise: flexibility, cardio, resistance, sports ...

Evening rituals: dinner, family, bed ...

To dos:

Delegated, postponed, declined:

Accomplishments

What, where, when, how, why, who was I today ...

Month _____ Day ___ Year _____

Spiritual: pray, praise, serve ...

Family: love, listen, laugh ...

Friends: reach out, encourage, share ...

Morning rituals: shower, dress, breakfast ...

Vitals: weight, blood pressure, etc.

Medical: medicines, treatments, etc.

Food & nutrition: morning, afternoon, evening (with calories) ...

Exercise: flexibility, cardio, resistance, sports ...

Evening rituals: dinner, family, bed ...

To dos:

Delegated, postponed, declined:

Accomplishments

What, where, when, how, why, who was I today ...

Spiritual: pray, praise, serve ...

Family: love, listen, laugh ...

Friends: reach out, encourage, share ...

Morning rituals: shower, dress, breakfast ...

Vitals: weight, blood pressure, etc.

Medical: medicines, treatments, etc.

Food & nutrition: morning, afternoon, evening (with calories) ...

Exercise: flexibility, cardio, resistance, sports ...

Evening rituals: dinner, family, bed ...

To dos:

Delegated, postponed, declined:

Accomplishments

What, where, when, how, why, who was I today ...

Month _____ Day ___ Year _____

Spiritual: pray, praise, serve ...

Family: love, listen, laugh ...

Friends: reach out, encourage, share ...

Morning rituals: shower, dress, breakfast ...

Vitals: weight, blood pressure, etc.

Medical: medicines, treatments, etc.

Food & nutrition: morning, afternoon, evening (with calories) ...

Exercise: flexibility, cardio, resistance, sports ...

Evening rituals: dinner, family, bed ...

To dos:

Delegated, postponed, declined:

Accomplishments

What, where, when, how, why, who was I today ...

Spiritual: pray, praise, serve ...

Family: love, listen, laugh ...

Friends: reach out, encourage, share ...

Morning rituals: shower, dress, breakfast ...

Vitals: weight, blood pressure, etc.

Medical: medicines, treatments, etc.

Food & nutrition: morning, afternoon, evening (with calories) ...

Exercise: flexibility, cardio, resistance, sports ...

Evening rituals: dinner, family, bed ...

To dos:

Delegated, postponed, declined:

Accomplishments

What, where, when, how, why, who was I today ...

Month _____ Day ___ Year _____

Spiritual: pray, praise, serve ...

Family: love, listen, laugh ...

Friends: reach out, encourage, share ...

Morning rituals: shower, dress, breakfast ...

Vitals: weight, blood pressure, etc.

Medical: medicines, treatments, etc.

Food & nutrition: morning, afternoon, evening (with calories) ...

Exercise: flexibility, cardio, resistance, sports ...

Evening rituals: dinner, family, bed ...

To dos:

Delegated, postponed, declined:

Accomplishments

What, where, when, how, why, who was I today ...

Month _____ Day ___ Year _____

Spiritual: pray, praise, serve ...

Family: love, listen, laugh ...

Friends: reach out, encourage, share ...

Morning rituals: shower, dress, breakfast ...

Vitals: weight, blood pressure, etc.

Medical: medicines, treatments, etc.

Food & nutrition: morning, afternoon, evening (with calories) ...

Exercise: flexibility, cardio, resistance, sports ...

Evening rituals: dinner, family, bed ...

To dos:

Delegated, postponed, declined:

Accomplishments

What, where, when, how, why, who was I today ...

Month _____ Day ___ Year _____

Spiritual: pray, praise, serve ...

Family: love, listen, laugh ...

Friends: reach out, encourage, share ...

Morning rituals: shower, dress, breakfast ...

Vitals: weight, blood pressure, etc.

Medical: medicines, treatments, etc.

Food & nutrition: morning, afternoon, evening (with calories) ...

Exercise: flexibility, cardio, resistance, sports ...

Evening rituals: dinner, family, bed ...

To dos:

Delegated, postponed, declined:

Accomplishments

What, where, when, how, why, who was I today ...

Month _____ Day ___ Year _____

Spiritual: pray, praise, serve ...

Family: love, listen, laugh ...

Friends: reach out, encourage, share ...

Morning rituals: shower, dress, breakfast ...

Vitals: weight, blood pressure, etc.

Medical: medicines, treatments, etc.

Food & nutrition: morning, afternoon, evening (with calories) ...

Exercise: flexibility, cardio, resistance, sports ...

Evening rituals: dinner, family, bed ...

To dos:

Delegated, postponed, declined:

Accomplishments

What, where, when, how, why, who was I today ...

Month _____ Day ___ Year _____

Spiritual: pray, praise, serve ...

Family: love, listen, laugh ...

Friends: reach out, encourage, share ...

Morning rituals: shower, dress, breakfast ...

Vitals: weight, blood pressure, etc.

Medical: medicines, treatments, etc.

Food & nutrition: morning, afternoon, evening (with calories) ...

Exercise: flexibility, cardio, resistance, sports ...

Evening rituals: dinner, family, bed ...

To dos:

Delegated, postponed, declined:

Accomplishments

What, where, when, how, why, who was I today ...

Month _____ Day ___ Year _____

Spiritual: pray, praise, serve ...

Family: love, listen, laugh ...

Friends: reach out, encourage, share ...

Morning rituals: shower, dress, breakfast ...

Vitals: weight, blood pressure, etc.

Medical: medicines, treatments, etc.

Food & nutrition: morning, afternoon, evening (with calories) ...

Exercise: flexibility, cardio, resistance, sports ...

Evening rituals: dinner, family, bed ...

To dos:

Delegated, postponed, declined:

Accomplishments

What, where, when, how, why, who was I today ...

Month _____ Day ___ Year _____

Spiritual: pray, praise, serve ...

Family: love, listen, laugh ...

Friends: reach out, encourage, share ...

Morning rituals: shower, dress, breakfast ...

Vitals: weight, blood pressure, etc.

Medical: medicines, treatments, etc.

Food & nutrition: morning, afternoon, evening (with calories) ...

Exercise: flexibility, cardio, resistance, sports ...

Evening rituals: dinner, family, bed ...

To dos:

Delegated, postponed, declined:

Accomplishments

What, where, when, how, why, who was I today ...

Month _____ Day ___ Year _____

Spiritual: pray, praise, serve ...

Family: love, listen, laugh ...

Friends: reach out, encourage, share ...

Morning rituals: shower, dress, breakfast ...

Vitals: weight, blood pressure, etc.

Medical: medicines, treatments, etc.

Food & nutrition: morning, afternoon, evening (with calories) ...

Exercise: flexibility, cardio, resistance, sports ...

Evening rituals: dinner, family, bed ...

To dos:

Delegated, postponed, declined:

Accomplishments

What, where, when, how, why, who was I today ...

Month _____ Day ___ Year _____

Spiritual: pray, praise, serve ...

Family: love, listen, laugh ...

Friends: reach out, encourage, share ...

Morning rituals: shower, dress, breakfast ...

Vitals: weight, blood pressure, etc.

Medical: medicines, treatments, etc.

Food & nutrition: morning, afternoon, evening (with calories) ...

Exercise: flexibility, cardio, resistance, sports ...

Evening rituals: dinner, family, bed ...

To dos:

Delegated, postponed, declined:

Accomplishments

What, where, when, how, why, who was I today ...

Month _____ Day ___ Year _____

Spiritual: pray, praise, serve ...

Family: love, listen, laugh ...

Friends: reach out, encourage, share ...

Morning rituals: shower, dress, breakfast ...

Vitals: weight, blood pressure, etc.

Medical: medicines, treatments, etc.

Food & nutrition: morning, afternoon, evening (with calories) ...

Exercise: flexibility, cardio, resistance, sports ...

Evening rituals: dinner, family, bed ...

To dos:

Delegated, postponed, declined:

Accomplishments

What, where, when, how, why, who was I today ...

Month _____ Day ___ Year _____

Spiritual: pray, praise, serve ...

Family: love, listen, laugh ...

Friends: reach out, encourage, share ...

Morning rituals: shower, dress, breakfast ...

Vitals: weight, blood pressure, etc.

Medical: medicines, treatments, etc.

Food & nutrition: morning, afternoon, evening (with calories) ...

Exercise: flexibility, cardio, resistance, sports ...

Evening rituals: dinner, family, bed ...

To dos:

Delegated, postponed, declined:

Accomplishments

What, where, when, how, why, who was I today ...

Month _____ Day ___ Year _____

Spiritual: pray, praise, serve ...

Family: love, listen, laugh ...

Friends: reach out, encourage, share ...

Morning rituals: shower, dress, breakfast ...

Vitals: weight, blood pressure, etc.

Medical: medicines, treatments, etc.

Food & nutrition: morning, afternoon, evening (with calories) ...

Exercise: flexibility, cardio, resistance, sports ...

Evening rituals: dinner, family, bed ...

To dos:

Delegated, postponed, declined:

Accomplishments

What, where, when, how, why, who was I today ...

Month _____ Day ___ Year _____

Spiritual: pray, praise, serve ...

Family: love, listen, laugh ...

Friends: reach out, encourage, share ...

Morning rituals: shower, dress, breakfast ...

Vitals: weight, blood pressure, etc.

Medical: medicines, treatments, etc.

Food & nutrition: morning, afternoon, evening (with calories) ...

Exercise: flexibility, cardio, resistance, sports ...

Evening rituals: dinner, family, bed ...

To dos:

Delegated, postponed, declined:

Accomplishments

What, where, when, how, why, who was I today ...

Month _____ Day ___ Year _____

Spiritual: pray, praise, serve ...

Family: love, listen, laugh ...

Friends: reach out, encourage, share ...

Morning rituals: shower, dress, breakfast ...

Vitals: weight, blood pressure, etc.

Medical: medicines, treatments, etc.

Food & nutrition: morning, afternoon, evening (with calories) ...

Exercise: flexibility, cardio, resistance, sports ...

Evening rituals: dinner, family, bed ...

To dos:

Delegated, postponed, declined:

Accomplishments

What, where, when, how, why, who was I today ...

Month _____ Day ___ Year _____

Spiritual: pray, praise, serve ...

Family: love, listen, laugh ...

Friends: reach out, encourage, share ...

Morning rituals: shower, dress, breakfast ...

Vitals: weight, blood pressure, etc.

Medical: medicines, treatments, etc.

Food & nutrition: morning, afternoon, evening (with calories) ...

Exercise: flexibility, cardio, resistance, sports ...

Evening rituals: dinner, family, bed ...

To dos:

Delegated, postponed, declined:

Accomplishments

What, where, when, how, why, who was I today ...

Month _____ Day ___ Year _____

Spiritual: pray, praise, serve ...

Family: love, listen, laugh ...

Friends: reach out, encourage, share ...

Morning rituals: shower, dress, breakfast ...

Vitals: weight, blood pressure, etc.

Medical: medicines, treatments, etc.

Food & nutrition: morning, afternoon, evening (with calories) ...

Exercise: flexibility, cardio, resistance, sports ...

Evening rituals: dinner, family, bed ...

To dos:

Delegated, postponed, declined:

Accomplishments

What, where, when, how, why, who was I today ...

Month _____ Day ___ Year _____

Spiritual: pray, praise, serve ...

Family: love, listen, laugh ...

Friends: reach out, encourage, share ...

Morning rituals: shower, dress, breakfast ...

Vitals: weight, blood pressure, etc.

Medical: medicines, treatments, etc.

Food & nutrition: morning, afternoon, evening (with calories) ...

Exercise: flexibility, cardio, resistance, sports ...

Evening rituals: dinner, family, bed ...

To dos:

Delegated, postponed, declined:

Accomplishments

What, where, when, how, why, who was I today ...

Month _____ Day ___ Year _____

Spiritual: pray, praise, serve ...

Family: love, listen, laugh ...

Friends: reach out, encourage, share ...

Morning rituals: shower, dress, breakfast ...

Vitals: weight, blood pressure, etc.

Medical: medicines, treatments, etc.

Food & nutrition: morning, afternoon, evening (with calories) ...

Exercise: flexibility, cardio, resistance, sports ...

Evening rituals: dinner, family, bed ...

To dos:

Delegated, postponed, declined:

Accomplishments

What, where, when, how, why, who was I today ...

Month _____ Day ___ Year _____

Spiritual: pray, praise, serve ...

Family: love, listen, laugh ...

Friends: reach out, encourage, share ...

Morning rituals: shower, dress, breakfast ...

Vitals: weight, blood pressure, etc.

Medical: medicines, treatments, etc.

Food & nutrition: morning, afternoon, evening (with calories) ...

Exercise: flexibility, cardio, resistance, sports ...

Evening rituals: dinner, family, bed ...

To dos:

Delegated, postponed, declined:

Accomplishments

What, where, when, how, why, who was I today ...

Month _____ Day ___ Year _____

Spiritual: pray, praise, serve ...

Family: love, listen, laugh ...

Friends: reach out, encourage, share ...

Morning rituals: shower, dress, breakfast ...

Vitals: weight, blood pressure, etc.

Medical: medicines, treatments, etc.

Food & nutrition: morning, afternoon, evening (with calories) ...

Exercise: flexibility, cardio, resistance, sports ...

Evening rituals: dinner, family, bed ...

To dos:

Delegated, postponed, declined:

Accomplishments

What, where, when, how, why, who was I today ...

Month _____ Day ___ Year _____

Spiritual: pray, praise, serve ...

Family: love, listen, laugh ...

Friends: reach out, encourage, share ...

Morning rituals: shower, dress, breakfast ...

Vitals: weight, blood pressure, etc.

Medical: medicines, treatments, etc.

Food & nutrition: morning, afternoon, evening (with calories) ...

Exercise: flexibility, cardio, resistance, sports ...

Evening rituals: dinner, family, bed ...

To dos:

Delegated, postponed, declined:

Accomplishments

What, where, when, how, why, who was I today ...

Month _____ Day ____ Year _____

Spiritual: pray, praise, serve ...

Family: love, listen, laugh ...

Friends: reach out, encourage, share ...

Morning rituals: shower, dress, breakfast ...

Vitals: weight, blood pressure, etc.

Medical: medicines, treatments, etc.

Food & nutrition: morning, afternoon, evening (with calories) ...

Exercise: flexibility, cardio, resistance, sports ...

Evening rituals: dinner, family, bed ...

To dos:

Delegated, postponed, declined:

Accomplishments

What, where, when, how, why, who was I today ...

Month _____ Day ___ Year _____

Spiritual: pray, praise, serve ...

Family: love, listen, laugh ...

Friends: reach out, encourage, share ...

Morning rituals: shower, dress, breakfast ...

Vitals: weight, blood pressure, etc.

Medical: medicines, treatments, etc.

Food & nutrition: morning, afternoon, evening (with calories) ...

Exercise: flexibility, cardio, resistance, sports ...

Evening rituals: dinner, family, bed ...

To dos:

Delegated, postponed, declined:

Accomplishments

What, where, when, how, why, who was I today ...

Month _____ Day ___ Year _____

Spiritual: pray, praise, serve ...

Family: love, listen, laugh ...

Friends: reach out, encourage, share ...

Morning rituals: shower, dress, breakfast ...

Vitals: weight, blood pressure, etc.

Medical: medicines, treatments, etc.

Food & nutrition: morning, afternoon, evening (with calories) ...

Exercise: flexibility, cardio, resistance, sports ...

Evening rituals: dinner, family, bed ...

To dos:

Delegated, postponed, declined:

Accomplishments

What, where, when, how, why, who was I today ...

Month _____ Day ___ Year _____

Spiritual: pray, praise, serve ...

Family: love, listen, laugh ...

Friends: reach out, encourage, share ...

Morning rituals: shower, dress, breakfast ...

Vitals: weight, blood pressure, etc.

Medical: medicines, treatments, etc.

Food & nutrition: morning, afternoon, evening (with calories) ...

Exercise: flexibility, cardio, resistance, sports ...

Evening rituals: dinner, family, bed ...

To dos:

Delegated, postponed, declined:

Accomplishments

What, where, when, how, why, who was I today ...

Month _____ Day ___ Year _____

Spiritual: pray, praise, serve ...

Family: love, listen, laugh ...

Friends: reach out, encourage, share ...

Morning rituals: shower, dress, breakfast ...

Vitals: weight, blood pressure, etc.

Medical: medicines, treatments, etc.

Food & nutrition: morning, afternoon, evening (with calories) ...

Exercise: flexibility, cardio, resistance, sports ...

Evening rituals: dinner, family, bed ...

To dos:

Delegated, postponed, declined:

Accomplishments

What, where, when, how, why, who was I today ...

Month _____ Day ___ Year _____

Spiritual: pray, praise, serve ...

Family: love, listen, laugh ...

Friends: reach out, encourage, share ...

Morning rituals: shower, dress, breakfast ...

Vitals: weight, blood pressure, etc.

Medical: medicines, treatments, etc.

Food & nutrition: morning, afternoon, evening (with calories) ...

Exercise: flexibility, cardio, resistance, sports ...

Evening rituals: dinner, family, bed ...

To dos:

Delegated, postponed, declined:

Accomplishments

What, where, when, how, why, who was I today ...

Spiritual: pray, praise, serve ...

Family: love, listen, laugh ...

Friends: reach out, encourage, share ...

Morning rituals: shower, dress, breakfast ...

Vitals: weight, blood pressure, etc.

Medical: medicines, treatments, etc.

Food & nutrition: morning, afternoon, evening (with calories) ...

Exercise: flexibility, cardio, resistance, sports ...

Evening rituals: dinner, family, bed ...

To dos:

Delegated, postponed, declined:

Accomplishments

What, where, when, how, why, who was I today ...

Month _____ Day ___ Year _____

Spiritual: pray, praise, serve ...

Family: love, listen, laugh ...

Friends: reach out, encourage, share ...

Morning rituals: shower, dress, breakfast ...

Vitals: weight, blood pressure, etc.

Medical: medicines, treatments, etc.

Food & nutrition: morning, afternoon, evening (with calories) ...

Exercise: flexibility, cardio, resistance, sports ...

Evening rituals: dinner, family, bed ...

To dos:

Delegated, postponed, declined:

Accomplishments

What, where, when, how, why, who was I today ...

Month _____ Day ___ Year _____

Spiritual: pray, praise, serve ...

Family: love, listen, laugh ...

Friends: reach out, encourage, share ...

Morning rituals: shower, dress, breakfast ...

Vitals: weight, blood pressure, etc.

Medical: medicines, treatments, etc.

Food & nutrition: morning, afternoon, evening (with calories) ...

Exercise: flexibility, cardio, resistance, sports ...

Evening rituals: dinner, family, bed ...

To dos:

Delegated, postponed, declined:

Accomplishments

What, where, when, how, why, who was I today ...

Month _____ Day ___ Year _____

Spiritual: pray, praise, serve ...

Family: love, listen, laugh ...

Friends: reach out, encourage, share ...

Morning rituals: shower, dress, breakfast ...

Vitals: weight, blood pressure, etc.

Medical: medicines, treatments, etc.

Food & nutrition: morning, afternoon, evening (with calories) ...

Exercise: flexibility, cardio, resistance, sports ...

Evening rituals: dinner, family, bed ...

To dos:

Delegated, postponed, declined:

Accomplishments

What, where, when, how, why, who was I today ...

Month _____ Day ___ Year _____

Spiritual: pray, praise, serve ...

Family: love, listen, laugh ...

Friends: reach out, encourage, share ...

Morning rituals: shower, dress, breakfast ...

Vitals: weight, blood pressure, etc.

Medical: medicines, treatments, etc.

Food & nutrition: morning, afternoon, evening (with calories) ...

Exercise: flexibility, cardio, resistance, sports ...

Evening rituals: dinner, family, bed ...

To dos:

Delegated, postponed, declined:

Accomplishments

What, where, when, how, why, who was I today ...

Month _____ Day ___ Year _____

Spiritual: pray, praise, serve ...

Family: love, listen, laugh ...

Friends: reach out, encourage, share ...

Morning rituals: shower, dress, breakfast ...

Vitals: weight, blood pressure, etc.

Medical: medicines, treatments, etc.

Food & nutrition: morning, afternoon, evening (with calories) ...

Exercise: flexibility, cardio, resistance, sports ...

Evening rituals: dinner, family, bed ...

To dos:

Delegated, postponed, declined:

Accomplishments

What, where, when, how, why, who was I today ...

Month _____ Day ___ Year _____

Spiritual: pray, praise, serve ...

Family: love, listen, laugh ...

Friends: reach out, encourage, share ...

Morning rituals: shower, dress, breakfast ...

Vitals: weight, blood pressure, etc.

Medical: medicines, treatments, etc.

Food & nutrition: morning, afternoon, evening (with calories) ...

Exercise: flexibility, cardio, resistance, sports ...

Evening rituals: dinner, family, bed ...

To dos:

Delegated, postponed, declined:

Accomplishments

What, where, when, how, why, who was I today ...

Month _____ Day ___ Year _____

Spiritual: pray, praise, serve ...

Family: love, listen, laugh ...

Friends: reach out, encourage, share ...

Morning rituals: shower, dress, breakfast ...

Vitals: weight, blood pressure, etc.

Medical: medicines, treatments, etc.

Food & nutrition: morning, afternoon, evening (with calories) ...

Exercise: flexibility, cardio, resistance, sports ...

Evening rituals: dinner, family, bed ...

To dos:

Delegated, postponed, declined:

Accomplishments

What, where, when, how, why, who was I today ...

Month _____ Day ___ Year _____

Spiritual: pray, praise, serve ...

Family: love, listen, laugh ...

Friends: reach out, encourage, share ...

Morning rituals: shower, dress, breakfast ...

Vitals: weight, blood pressure, etc.

Medical: medicines, treatments, etc.

Food & nutrition: morning, afternoon, evening (with calories) ...

Exercise: flexibility, cardio, resistance, sports ...

Evening rituals: dinner, family, bed ...

To dos:

Delegated, postponed, declined:

Accomplishments

What, where, when, how, why, who was I today ...

Month _____ Day ___ Year _____

Spiritual: pray, praise, serve ...

Family: love, listen, laugh ...

Friends: reach out, encourage, share ...

Morning rituals: shower, dress, breakfast ...

Vitals: weight, blood pressure, etc.

Medical: medicines, treatments, etc.

Food & nutrition: morning, afternoon, evening (with calories) ...

Exercise: flexibility, cardio, resistance, sports ...

Evening rituals: dinner, family, bed ...

To dos:

Delegated, postponed, declined:

Accomplishments

What, where, when, how, why, who was I today ...

Month _____ Day ___ Year _____

Spiritual: pray, praise, serve ...

Family: love, listen, laugh ...

Friends: reach out, encourage, share ...

Morning rituals: shower, dress, breakfast ...

Vitals: weight, blood pressure, etc.

Medical: medicines, treatments, etc.

Food & nutrition: morning, afternoon, evening (with calories) ...

Exercise: flexibility, cardio, resistance, sports ...

Evening rituals: dinner, family, bed ...

To dos:

Delegated, postponed, declined:

Accomplishments

What, where, when, how, why, who was I today ...

Month _____ Day ___ Year _____

Spiritual: pray, praise, serve ...

Family: love, listen, laugh ...

Friends: reach out, encourage, share ...

Morning rituals: shower, dress, breakfast ...

Vitals: weight, blood pressure, etc.

Medical: medicines, treatments, etc.

Food & nutrition: morning, afternoon, evening (with calories) ...

Exercise: flexibility, cardio, resistance, sports ...

Evening rituals: dinner, family, bed ...

To dos:

Delegated, postponed, declined:

Accomplishments

What, where, when, how, why, who was I today ...

Month _____ Day ____ Year _____

Spiritual: pray, praise, serve ...

Family: love, listen, laugh ...

Friends: reach out, encourage, share ...

Morning rituals: shower, dress, breakfast ...

Vitals: weight, blood pressure, etc.

Medical: medicines, treatments, etc.

Food & nutrition: morning, afternoon, evening (with calories) ...

Exercise: flexibility, cardio, resistance, sports ...

Evening rituals: dinner, family, bed ...

To dos:

Delegated, postponed, declined:

Accomplishments

What, where, when, how, why, who was I today ...

Month _____ Day ___ Year _____

Spiritual: pray, praise, serve ...

Family: love, listen, laugh ...

Friends: reach out, encourage, share ...

Morning rituals: shower, dress, breakfast ...

Vitals: weight, blood pressure, etc.

Medical: medicines, treatments, etc.

Food & nutrition: morning, afternoon, evening (with calories) ...

Exercise: flexibility, cardio, resistance, sports ...

Evening rituals: dinner, family, bed ...

To dos:

Delegated, postponed, declined:

Accomplishments

What, where, when, how, why, who was I today ...

Month _____ Day ___ Year _____

Spiritual: pray, praise, serve ...

Family: love, listen, laugh ...

Friends: reach out, encourage, share ...

Morning rituals: shower, dress, breakfast ...

Vitals: weight, blood pressure, etc.

Medical: medicines, treatments, etc.

Food & nutrition: morning, afternoon, evening (with calories) ...

Exercise: flexibility, cardio, resistance, sports ...

Evening rituals: dinner, family, bed ...

To dos:

Delegated, postponed, declined:

Accomplishments

What, where, when, how, why, who was I today ...

Month _____ Day ___ Year _____

Spiritual: pray, praise, serve ...

Family: love, listen, laugh ...

Friends: reach out, encourage, share ...

Morning rituals: shower, dress, breakfast ...

Vitals: weight, blood pressure, etc.

Medical: medicines, treatments, etc.

Food & nutrition: morning, afternoon, evening (with calories) ...

Exercise: flexibility, cardio, resistance, sports ...

Evening rituals: dinner, family, bed ...

To dos:

Delegated, postponed, declined:

Accomplishments

What, where, when, how, why, who was I today ...

Month _____ Day ___ Year _____

Spiritual: pray, praise, serve ...

Family: love, listen, laugh ...

Friends: reach out, encourage, share ...

Morning rituals: shower, dress, breakfast ...

Vitals: weight, blood pressure, etc.

Medical: medicines, treatments, etc.

Food & nutrition: morning, afternoon, evening (with calories) ...

Exercise: flexibility, cardio, resistance, sports ...

Evening rituals: dinner, family, bed ...

To dos:

Delegated, postponed, declined:

Accomplishments

What, where, when, how, why, who was I today ...

Month _____ Day ___ Year _____

Spiritual: pray, praise, serve ...

Family: love, listen, laugh ...

Friends: reach out, encourage, share ...

Morning rituals: shower, dress, breakfast ...

Vitals: weight, blood pressure, etc.

Medical: medicines, treatments, etc.

Food & nutrition: morning, afternoon, evening (with calories) ...

Exercise: flexibility, cardio, resistance, sports ...

Evening rituals: dinner, family, bed ...

To dos:

Delegated, postponed, declined:

Accomplishments

What, where, when, how, why, who was I today ...

Month _____ Day ___ Year _____

Spiritual: pray, praise, serve ...

Family: love, listen, laugh ...

Friends: reach out, encourage, share ...

Morning rituals: shower, dress, breakfast ...

Vitals: weight, blood pressure, etc.

Medical: medicines, treatments, etc.

Food & nutrition: morning, afternoon, evening (with calories) ...

Exercise: flexibility, cardio, resistance, sports ...

Evening rituals: dinner, family, bed ...

To dos:

Delegated, postponed, declined:

Accomplishments

What, where, when, how, why, who was I today ...

Month _____ Day ___ Year _____

Spiritual: pray, praise, serve ...

Family: love, listen, laugh ...

Friends: reach out, encourage, share ...

Morning rituals: shower, dress, breakfast ...

Vitals: weight, blood pressure, etc.

Medical: medicines, treatments, etc.

Food & nutrition: morning, afternoon, evening (with calories) ...

Exercise: flexibility, cardio, resistance, sports ...

Evening rituals: dinner, family, bed ...

To dos:

Delegated, postponed, declined:

Accomplishments

What, where, when, how, why, who was I today ...

Month _____ Day ___ Year _____

Spiritual: pray, praise, serve ...

Family: love, listen, laugh ...

Friends: reach out, encourage, share ...

Morning rituals: shower, dress, breakfast ...

Vitals: weight, blood pressure, etc.

Medical: medicines, treatments, etc.

Food & nutrition: morning, afternoon, evening (with calories) ...

Exercise: flexibility, cardio, resistance, sports ...

Evening rituals: dinner, family, bed ...

To dos:

Delegated, postponed, declined:

Accomplishments

What, where, when, how, why, who was I today ...

Month _____ Day ___ Year ____

Spiritual: pray, praise, serve ...

Family: love, listen, laugh ...

Friends: reach out, encourage, share ...

Morning rituals: shower, dress, breakfast ...

Vitals: weight, blood pressure, etc.

Medical: medicines, treatments, etc.

Food & nutrition: morning, afternoon, evening (with calories) ...

Exercise: flexibility, cardio, resistance, sports ...

Evening rituals: dinner, family, bed ...

To dos:

Delegated, postponed, declined:

Accomplishments

What, where, when, how, why, who was I today ...

Spiritual: pray, praise, serve ...

Family: love, listen, laugh ...

Friends: reach out, encourage, share ...

Morning rituals: shower, dress, breakfast ...

Vitals: weight, blood pressure, etc.

Medical: medicines, treatments, etc.

Food & nutrition: morning, afternoon, evening (with calories) ...

Exercise: flexibility, cardio, resistance, sports ...

Evening rituals: dinner, family, bed ...

To dos:

Delegated, postponed, declined:

Accomplishments

What, where, when, how, why, who was I today ...

Month _____ Day ___ Year _____

Spiritual: pray, praise, serve ...

Family: love, listen, laugh ...

Friends: reach out, encourage, share ...

Morning rituals: shower, dress, breakfast ...

Vitals: weight, blood pressure, etc.

Medical: medicines, treatments, etc.

Food & nutrition: morning, afternoon, evening (with calories) ...

Exercise: flexibility, cardio, resistance, sports ...

Evening rituals: dinner, family, bed ...

To dos:

Delegated, postponed, declined:

Accomplishments

What, where, when, how, why, who was I today ...

Spiritual: pray, praise, serve ...

Family: love, listen, laugh ...

Friends: reach out, encourage, share ...

Morning rituals: shower, dress, breakfast ...

Vitals: weight, blood pressure, etc.

Medical: medicines, treatments, etc.

Food & nutrition: morning, afternoon, evening (with calories) ...

Exercise: flexibility, cardio, resistance, sports ...

Evening rituals: dinner, family, bed ...

To dos:

Delegated, postponed, declined:

Accomplishments

What, where, when, how, why, who was I today ...

Month _____ Day ___ Year _____

Spiritual: pray, praise, serve ...

Family: love, listen, laugh ...

Friends: reach out, encourage, share ...

Morning rituals: shower, dress, breakfast ...

Vitals: weight, blood pressure, etc.

Medical: medicines, treatments, etc.

Food & nutrition: morning, afternoon, evening (with calories) ...

Exercise: flexibility, cardio, resistance, sports ...

Evening rituals: dinner, family, bed ...

To dos:

Delegated, postponed, declined:

Accomplishments

What, where, when, how, why, who was I today ...

Spiritual: pray, praise, serve ...

Family: love, listen, laugh ...

Friends: reach out, encourage, share ...

Morning rituals: shower, dress, breakfast ...

Vitals: weight, blood pressure, etc.

Medical: medicines, treatments, etc.

Food & nutrition: morning, afternoon, evening (with calories) ...

Exercise: flexibility, cardio, resistance, sports ...

Evening rituals: dinner, family, bed ...

To dos:

Delegated, postponed, declined:

Accomplishments

What, where, when, how, why, who was I today ...

Month _____ Day ___ Year _____

Spiritual: pray, praise, serve ...

Family: love, listen, laugh ...

Friends: reach out, encourage, share ...

Morning rituals: shower, dress, breakfast ...

Vitals: weight, blood pressure, etc.

Medical: medicines, treatments, etc.

Food & nutrition: morning, afternoon, evening (with calories) ...

Exercise: flexibility, cardio, resistance, sports ...

Evening rituals: dinner, family, bed ...

To dos:

Delegated, postponed, declined:

Accomplishments

What, where, when, how, why, who was I today ...

Month _____ Day ___ Year _____

Spiritual: pray, praise, serve ...

Family: love, listen, laugh ...

Friends: reach out, encourage, share ...

Morning rituals: shower, dress, breakfast ...

Vitals: weight, blood pressure, etc.

Medical: medicines, treatments, etc.

Food & nutrition: morning, afternoon, evening (with calories) ...

Exercise: flexibility, cardio, resistance, sports ...

Evening rituals: dinner, family, bed ...

To dos:

Delegated, postponed, declined:

Accomplishments

What, where, when, how, why, who was I today ...

Month _____ Day ___ Year _____

Spiritual: pray, praise, serve ...

Family: love, listen, laugh ...

Friends: reach out, encourage, share ...

Morning rituals: shower, dress, breakfast ...

Vitals: weight, blood pressure, etc.

Medical: medicines, treatments, etc.

Food & nutrition: morning, afternoon, evening (with calories) ...

Exercise: flexibility, cardio, resistance, sports ...

Evening rituals: dinner, family, bed ...

To dos:

Delegated, postponed, declined:

Accomplishments

What, where, when, how, why, who was I today ...

Month _____ Day ___ Year _____

Spiritual: pray, praise, serve ...

Family: love, listen, laugh ...

Friends: reach out, encourage, share ...

Morning rituals: shower, dress, breakfast ...

Vitals: weight, blood pressure, etc.

Medical: medicines, treatments, etc.

Food & nutrition: morning, afternoon, evening (with calories) ...

Exercise: flexibility, cardio, resistance, sports ...

Evening rituals: dinner, family, bed ...

To dos:

Delegated, postponed, declined:

Accomplishments

What, where, when, how, why, who was I today ...

Month _____ Day ___ Year _____

Spiritual: pray, praise, serve ...

Family: love, listen, laugh ...

Friends: reach out, encourage, share ...

Morning rituals: shower, dress, breakfast ...

Vitals: weight, blood pressure, etc.

Medical: medicines, treatments, etc.

Food & nutrition: morning, afternoon, evening (with calories) ...

Exercise: flexibility, cardio, resistance, sports ...

Evening rituals: dinner, family, bed ...

To dos:

Delegated, postponed, declined:

Accomplishments

What, where, when, how, why, who was I today ...

Month _____ Day ___ Year _____

Spiritual: pray, praise, serve ...

Family: love, listen, laugh ...

Friends: reach out, encourage, share ...

Morning rituals: shower, dress, breakfast ...

Vitals: weight, blood pressure, etc.

Medical: medicines, treatments, etc.

Food & nutrition: morning, afternoon, evening (with calories) ...

Exercise: flexibility, cardio, resistance, sports ...

Evening rituals: dinner, family, bed ...

To dos:

Delegated, postponed, declined:

Accomplishments

What, where, when, how, why, who was I today ...

Month _____ Day ___ Year _____

Spiritual: pray, praise, serve ...

Family: love, listen, laugh ...

Friends: reach out, encourage, share ...

Morning rituals: shower, dress, breakfast ...

Vitals: weight, blood pressure, etc.

Medical: medicines, treatments, etc.

Food & nutrition: morning, afternoon, evening (with calories) ...

Exercise: flexibility, cardio, resistance, sports ...

Evening rituals: dinner, family, bed ...

To dos:

Delegated, postponed, declined:

Accomplishments

What, where, when, how, why, who was I today ...

Month _____ Day ___ Year _____

Spiritual: pray, praise, serve ...

Family: love, listen, laugh ...

Friends: reach out, encourage, share ...

Morning rituals: shower, dress, breakfast ...

Vitals: weight, blood pressure, etc.

Medical: medicines, treatments, etc.

Food & nutrition: morning, afternoon, evening (with calories) ...

Exercise: flexibility, cardio, resistance, sports ...

Evening rituals: dinner, family, bed ...

To dos:

Delegated, postponed, declined:

Accomplishments

What, where, when, how, why, who was I today ...

Month _____ Day ___ Year _____

Spiritual: pray, praise, serve ...

Family: love, listen, laugh ...

Friends: reach out, encourage, share ...

Morning rituals: shower, dress, breakfast ...

Vitals: weight, blood pressure, etc.

Medical: medicines, treatments, etc.

Food & nutrition: morning, afternoon, evening (with calories) ...

Exercise: flexibility, cardio, resistance, sports ...

Evening rituals: dinner, family, bed ...

To dos:

Delegated, postponed, declined:

Accomplishments

What, where, when, how, why, who was I today ...

Month _____ Day ___ Year _____

Spiritual: pray, praise, serve ...

Family: love, listen, laugh ...

Friends: reach out, encourage, share ...

Morning rituals: shower, dress, breakfast ...

Vitals: weight, blood pressure, etc.

Medical: medicines, treatments, etc.

Food & nutrition: morning, afternoon, evening (with calories) ...

Exercise: flexibility, cardio, resistance, sports ...

Evening rituals: dinner, family, bed ...

To dos:

Delegated, postponed, declined:

Accomplishments

What, where, when, how, why, who was I today ...

Month _____ Day ___ Year _____

Spiritual: pray, praise, serve ...

Family: love, listen, laugh ...

Friends: reach out, encourage, share ...

Morning rituals: shower, dress, breakfast ...

Vitals: weight, blood pressure, etc.

Medical: medicines, treatments, etc.

Food & nutrition: morning, afternoon, evening (with calories) ...

Exercise: flexibility, cardio, resistance, sports ...

Evening rituals: dinner, family, bed ...

To dos:

Delegated, postponed, declined:

Accomplishments

What, where, when, how, why, who was I today ...

Month _____ Day ___ Year _____

Spiritual: pray, praise, serve ...

Family: love, listen, laugh ...

Friends: reach out, encourage, share ...

Morning rituals: shower, dress, breakfast ...

Vitals: weight, blood pressure, etc.

Medical: medicines, treatments, etc.

Food & nutrition: morning, afternoon, evening (with calories) ...

Exercise: flexibility, cardio, resistance, sports ...

Evening rituals: dinner, family, bed ...

To dos:

Delegated, postponed, declined:

Accomplishments

What, where, when, how, why, who was I today ...

Month _____ Day ___ Year _____

Spiritual: pray, praise, serve ...

Family: love, listen, laugh ...

Friends: reach out, encourage, share ...

Morning rituals: shower, dress, breakfast ...

Vitals: weight, blood pressure, etc.

Medical: medicines, treatments, etc.

Food & nutrition: morning, afternoon, evening (with calories) ...

Exercise: flexibility, cardio, resistance, sports ...

Evening rituals: dinner, family, bed ...

To dos:

Delegated, postponed, declined:

Accomplishments

What, where, when, how, why, who was I today ...

Spiritual: pray, praise, serve ...

Family: love, listen, laugh ...

Friends: reach out, encourage, share ...

Morning rituals: shower, dress, breakfast ...

Vitals: weight, blood pressure, etc.

Medical: medicines, treatments, etc.

Food & nutrition: morning, afternoon, evening (with calories) ...

Exercise: flexibility, cardio, resistance, sports ...

Evening rituals: dinner, family, bed ...

To dos:

Delegated, postponed, declined:

Accomplishments

What, where, when, how, why, who was I today ...

Month _____ Day ___ Year _____

Spiritual: pray, praise, serve ...

Family: love, listen, laugh ...

Friends: reach out, encourage, share ...

Morning rituals: shower, dress, breakfast ...

Vitals: weight, blood pressure, etc.

Medical: medicines, treatments, etc.

Food & nutrition: morning, afternoon, evening (with calories) ...

Exercise: flexibility, cardio, resistance, sports ...

Evening rituals: dinner, family, bed ...

To dos:

Delegated, postponed, declined:

Accomplishments

What, where, when, how, why, who was I today ...

Month _____ Day ____ Year _____

Spiritual: pray, praise, serve ...

Family: love, listen, laugh ...

Friends: reach out, encourage, share ...

Morning rituals: shower, dress, breakfast ...

Vitals: weight, blood pressure, etc.

Medical: medicines, treatments, etc.

Food & nutrition: morning, afternoon, evening (with calories) ...

Exercise: flexibility, cardio, resistance, sports ...

Evening rituals: dinner, family, bed ...

To dos:

Delegated, postponed, declined:

Accomplishments

What, where, when, how, why, who was I today ...

Month _____ Day ___ Year _____

Spiritual: pray, praise, serve ...

Family: love, listen, laugh ...

Friends: reach out, encourage, share ...

Morning rituals: shower, dress, breakfast ...

Vitals: weight, blood pressure, etc.

Medical: medicines, treatments, etc.

Food & nutrition: morning, afternoon, evening (with calories) ...

Exercise: flexibility, cardio, resistance, sports ...

Evening rituals: dinner, family, bed ...

To dos:

Delegated, postponed, declined:

Accomplishments

What, where, when, how, why, who was I today ...

Month _____ Day ___ Year _____

Spiritual: pray, praise, serve ...

Family: love, listen, laugh ...

Friends: reach out, encourage, share ...

Morning rituals: shower, dress, breakfast ...

Vitals: weight, blood pressure, etc.

Medical: medicines, treatments, etc.

Food & nutrition: morning, afternoon, evening (with calories) ...

Exercise: flexibility, cardio, resistance, sports ...

Evening rituals: dinner, family, bed ...

To dos:

Delegated, postponed, declined:

Accomplishments

What, where, when, how, why, who was I today ...

Month _____ Day ___ Year _____

Spiritual: pray, praise, serve ...

Family: love, listen, laugh ...

Friends: reach out, encourage, share ...

Morning rituals: shower, dress, breakfast ...

Vitals: weight, blood pressure, etc.

Medical: medicines, treatments, etc.

Food & nutrition: morning, afternoon, evening (with calories) ...

Exercise: flexibility, cardio, resistance, sports ...

Evening rituals: dinner, family, bed ...

To dos:

Delegated, postponed, declined:

Accomplishments

What, where, when, how, why, who was I today ...

Month _____ Day ___ Year _____

Spiritual: pray, praise, serve ...

Family: love, listen, laugh ...

Friends: reach out, encourage, share ...

Morning rituals: shower, dress, breakfast ...

Vitals: weight, blood pressure, etc.

Medical: medicines, treatments, etc.

Food & nutrition: morning, afternoon, evening (with calories) ...

Exercise: flexibility, cardio, resistance, sports ...

Evening rituals: dinner, family, bed ...

To dos:

Delegated, postponed, declined:

Accomplishments

What, where, when, how, why, who was I today ...

Month _____ Day ___ Year _____

Spiritual: pray, praise, serve ...

Family: love, listen, laugh ...

Friends: reach out, encourage, share ...

Morning rituals: shower, dress, breakfast ...

Vitals: weight, blood pressure, etc.

Medical: medicines, treatments, etc.

Food & nutrition: morning, afternoon, evening (with calories) ...

Exercise: flexibility, cardio, resistance, sports ...

Evening rituals: dinner, family, bed ...

To dos:

Delegated, postponed, declined:

Accomplishments

What, where, when, how, why, who was I today ...

Spiritual: pray, praise, serve ...

Family: love, listen, laugh ...

Friends: reach out, encourage, share ...

Morning rituals: shower, dress, breakfast ...

Vitals: weight, blood pressure, etc.

Medical: medicines, treatments, etc.

Food & nutrition: morning, afternoon, evening (with calories) ...

Exercise: flexibility, cardio, resistance, sports ...

Evening rituals: dinner, family, bed ...

To dos:

Delegated, postponed, declined:

Accomplishments

What, where, when, how, why, who was I today ...

Month _____ Day ___ Year ____

Spiritual: pray, praise, serve ...

Family: love, listen, laugh ...

Friends: reach out, encourage, share ...

Morning rituals: shower, dress, breakfast ...

Vitals: weight, blood pressure, etc.

Medical: medicines, treatments, etc.

Food & nutrition: morning, afternoon, evening (with calories) ...

Exercise: flexibility, cardio, resistance, sports ...

Evening rituals: dinner, family, bed ...

To dos:

Delegated, postponed, declined:

Accomplishments

What, where, when, how, why, who was I today ...

Month _____ Day ___ Year _____

Spiritual: pray, praise, serve ...

Family: love, listen, laugh ...

Friends: reach out, encourage, share ...

Morning rituals: shower, dress, breakfast ...

Vitals: weight, blood pressure, etc.

Medical: medicines, treatments, etc.

Food & nutrition: morning, afternoon, evening (with calories) ...

Exercise: flexibility, cardio, resistance, sports ...

Evening rituals: dinner, family, bed ...

To dos:

Delegated, postponed, declined:

Accomplishments

What, where, when, how, why, who was I today ...

Month _____ Day ___ Year _____

Spiritual: pray, praise, serve ...

Family: love, listen, laugh ...

Friends: reach out, encourage, share ...

Morning rituals: shower, dress, breakfast ...

Vitals: weight, blood pressure, etc.

Medical: medicines, treatments, etc.

Food & nutrition: morning, afternoon, evening (with calories) ...

Exercise: flexibility, cardio, resistance, sports ...

Evening rituals: dinner, family, bed ...

To dos:

Delegated, postponed, declined:

Accomplishments

What, where, when, how, why, who was I today ...

Month _____ Day ___ Year _____

Spiritual: pray, praise, serve ...

Family: love, listen, laugh ...

Friends: reach out, encourage, share ...

Morning rituals: shower, dress, breakfast ...

Vitals: weight, blood pressure, etc.

Medical: medicines, treatments, etc.

Food & nutrition: morning, afternoon, evening (with calories) ...

Exercise: flexibility, cardio, resistance, sports ...

Evening rituals: dinner, family, bed ...

To dos:

Delegated, postponed, declined:

Accomplishments

What, where, when, how, why, who was I today ...

Month _____ Day ___ Year _____

Spiritual: pray, praise, serve ...

Family: love, listen, laugh ...

Friends: reach out, encourage, share ...

Morning rituals: shower, dress, breakfast ...

Vitals: weight, blood pressure, etc.

Medical: medicines, treatments, etc.

Food & nutrition: morning, afternoon, evening (with calories) ...

Exercise: flexibility, cardio, resistance, sports ...

Evening rituals: dinner, family, bed ...

To dos:

Delegated, postponed, declined:

Accomplishments

What, where, when, how, why, who was I today ...

Month _____ Day ____ Year _____

Spiritual: pray, praise, serve ...

Family: love, listen, laugh ...

Friends: reach out, encourage, share ...

Morning rituals: shower, dress, breakfast ...

Vitals: weight, blood pressure, etc.

Medical: medicines, treatments, etc.

Food & nutrition: morning, afternoon, evening (with calories) ...

Exercise: flexibility, cardio, resistance, sports ...

Evening rituals: dinner, family, bed ...

To dos:

Delegated, postponed, declined:

Accomplishments

What, where, when, how, why, who was I today ...

Month _____ Day ___ Year _____

Spiritual: pray, praise, serve ...

Family: love, listen, laugh ...

Friends: reach out, encourage, share ...

Morning rituals: shower, dress, breakfast ...

Vitals: weight, blood pressure, etc.

Medical: medicines, treatments, etc.

Food & nutrition: morning, afternoon, evening (with calories) ...

Exercise: flexibility, cardio, resistance, sports ...

Evening rituals: dinner, family, bed ...

To dos:

Delegated, postponed, declined:

Accomplishments

What, where, when, how, why, who was I today ...

Month _____ Day ___ Year _____

Spiritual: pray, praise, serve ...

Family: love, listen, laugh ...

Friends: reach out, encourage, share ...

Morning rituals: shower, dress, breakfast ...

Vitals: weight, blood pressure, etc.

Medical: medicines, treatments, etc.

Food & nutrition: morning, afternoon, evening (with calories) ...

Exercise: flexibility, cardio, resistance, sports ...

Evening rituals: dinner, family, bed ...

To dos:

Delegated, postponed, declined:

Accomplishments

What, where, when, how, why, who was I today ...

Month _____ Day ___ Year ____

Spiritual: pray, praise, serve ...

Family: love, listen, laugh ...

Friends: reach out, encourage, share ...

Morning rituals: shower, dress, breakfast ...

Vitals: weight, blood pressure, etc.

Medical: medicines, treatments, etc.

Food & nutrition: morning, afternoon, evening (with calories) ...

Exercise: flexibility, cardio, resistance, sports ...

Evening rituals: dinner, family, bed ...

To dos:

Delegated, postponed, declined:

Accomplishments

What, where, when, how, why, who was I today ...

Spiritual: pray, praise, serve ...

Family: love, listen, laugh ...

Friends: reach out, encourage, share ...

Morning rituals: shower, dress, breakfast ...

Vitals: weight, blood pressure, etc.

Medical: medicines, treatments, etc.

Food & nutrition: morning, afternoon, evening (with calories) ...

Exercise: flexibility, cardio, resistance, sports ...

Evening rituals: dinner, family, bed ...

To dos:

Delegated, postponed, declined:

Accomplishments

What, where, when, how, why, who was I today ...

Month _____ Day ___ Year _____

Spiritual: pray, praise, serve ...

Family: love, listen, laugh ...

Friends: reach out, encourage, share ...

Morning rituals: shower, dress, breakfast ...

Vitals: weight, blood pressure, etc.

Medical: medicines, treatments, etc.

Food & nutrition: morning, afternoon, evening (with calories) ...

Exercise: flexibility, cardio, resistance, sports ...

Evening rituals: dinner, family, bed ...

To dos:

Delegated, postponed, declined:

Accomplishments

What, where, when, how, why, who was I today ...

Month _____ Day ___ Year _____

Spiritual: pray, praise, serve ...

Family: love, listen, laugh ...

Friends: reach out, encourage, share ...

Morning rituals: shower, dress, breakfast ...

Vitals: weight, blood pressure, etc.

Medical: medicines, treatments, etc.

Food & nutrition: morning, afternoon, evening (with calories) ...

Exercise: flexibility, cardio, resistance, sports ...

Evening rituals: dinner, family, bed ...

To dos:

Delegated, postponed, declined:

Accomplishments

What, where, when, how, why, who was I today ...

Month _____ Day ___ Year _____

Spiritual: pray, praise, serve ...

Family: love, listen, laugh ...

Friends: reach out, encourage, share ...

Morning rituals: shower, dress, breakfast ...

Vitals: weight, blood pressure, etc.

Medical: medicines, treatments, etc.

Food & nutrition: morning, afternoon, evening (with calories) ...

Exercise: flexibility, cardio, resistance, sports ...

Evening rituals: dinner, family, bed ...

To dos:

Delegated, postponed, declined:

Accomplishments

What, where, when, how, why, who was I today ...

Month _____ Day ___ Year ____

Spiritual: pray, praise, serve ...

Family: love, listen, laugh ...

Friends: reach out, encourage, share ...

Morning rituals: shower, dress, breakfast ...

Vitals: weight, blood pressure, etc.

Medical: medicines, treatments, etc.

Food & nutrition: morning, afternoon, evening (with calories) ...

Exercise: flexibility, cardio, resistance, sports ...

Evening rituals: dinner, family, bed ...

To dos:

Delegated, postponed, declined:

Accomplishments

What, where, when, how, why, who was I today ...

Month _____ Day ___ Year _____

Spiritual: pray, praise, serve ...

Family: love, listen, laugh ...

Friends: reach out, encourage, share ...

Morning rituals: shower, dress, breakfast ...

Vitals: weight, blood pressure, etc.

Medical: medicines, treatments, etc.

Food & nutrition: morning, afternoon, evening (with calories) ...

Exercise: flexibility, cardio, resistance, sports ...

Evening rituals: dinner, family, bed ...

To dos:

Delegated, postponed, declined:

Accomplishments

What, where, when, how, why, who was I today ...

Month _____ Day ___ Year _____

Spiritual: pray, praise, serve ...

Family: love, listen, laugh ...

Friends: reach out, encourage, share ...

Morning rituals: shower, dress, breakfast ...

Vitals: weight, blood pressure, etc.

Medical: medicines, treatments, etc.

Food & nutrition: morning, afternoon, evening (with calories) ...

Exercise: flexibility, cardio, resistance, sports ...

Evening rituals: dinner, family, bed ...

To dos:

Delegated, postponed, declined:

Accomplishments

What, where, when, how, why, who was I today ...

Month _____ Day ___ Year _____

Spiritual: pray, praise, serve ...

Family: love, listen, laugh ...

Friends: reach out, encourage, share ...

Morning rituals: shower, dress, breakfast ...

Vitals: weight, blood pressure, etc.

Medical: medicines, treatments, etc.

Food & nutrition: morning, afternoon, evening (with calories) ...

Exercise: flexibility, cardio, resistance, sports ...

Evening rituals: dinner, family, bed ...

To dos:

Delegated, postponed, declined:

Accomplishments

What, where, when, how, why, who was I today ...

Spiritual: pray, praise, serve ...

Family: love, listen, laugh ...

Friends: reach out, encourage, share ...

Morning rituals: shower, dress, breakfast ...

Vitals: weight, blood pressure, etc.

Medical: medicines, treatments, etc.

Food & nutrition: morning, afternoon, evening (with calories) ...

Exercise: flexibility, cardio, resistance, sports ...

Evening rituals: dinner, family, bed ...

To dos:

Delegated, postponed, declined:

Accomplishments

What, where, when, how, why, who was I today ...

Month _____ Day ___ Year _____

Spiritual: pray, praise, serve ...

Family: love, listen, laugh ...

Friends: reach out, encourage, share ...

Morning rituals: shower, dress, breakfast ...

Vitals: weight, blood pressure, etc.

Medical: medicines, treatments, etc.

Food & nutrition: morning, afternoon, evening (with calories) ...

Exercise: flexibility, cardio, resistance, sports ...

Evening rituals: dinner, family, bed ...

To dos:

Delegated, postponed, declined:

Accomplishments

What, where, when, how, why, who was I today ...

Month _____ Day ___ Year _____

Spiritual: pray, praise, serve ...

Family: love, listen, laugh ...

Friends: reach out, encourage, share ...

Morning rituals: shower, dress, breakfast ...

Vitals: weight, blood pressure, etc.

Medical: medicines, treatments, etc.

Food & nutrition: morning, afternoon, evening (with calories) ...

Exercise: flexibility, cardio, resistance, sports ...

Evening rituals: dinner, family, bed ...

To dos:

Delegated, postponed, declined:

Accomplishments

What, where, when, how, why, who was I today ...

Month _____ Day ___ Year _____

Spiritual: pray, praise, serve ...

Family: love, listen, laugh ...

Friends: reach out, encourage, share ...

Morning rituals: shower, dress, breakfast ...

Vitals: weight, blood pressure, etc.

Medical: medicines, treatments, etc.

Food & nutrition: morning, afternoon, evening (with calories) ...

Exercise: flexibility, cardio, resistance, sports ...

Evening rituals: dinner, family, bed ...

To dos:

Delegated, postponed, declined:

Accomplishments

What, where, when, how, why, who was I today ...

Month _____ Day ___ Year _____

Spiritual: pray, praise, serve ...

Family: love, listen, laugh ...

Friends: reach out, encourage, share ...

Morning rituals: shower, dress, breakfast ...

Vitals: weight, blood pressure, etc.

Medical: medicines, treatments, etc.

Food & nutrition: morning, afternoon, evening (with calories) ...

Exercise: flexibility, cardio, resistance, sports ...

Evening rituals: dinner, family, bed ...

To dos:

Delegated, postponed, declined:

Accomplishments

What, where, when, how, why, who was I today ...

Month _____ Day ___ Year _____

Spiritual: pray, praise, serve ...

Family: love, listen, laugh ...

Friends: reach out, encourage, share ...

Morning rituals: shower, dress, breakfast ...

Vitals: weight, blood pressure, etc.

Medical: medicines, treatments, etc.

Food & nutrition: morning, afternoon, evening (with calories) ...

Exercise: flexibility, cardio, resistance, sports ...

Evening rituals: dinner, family, bed ...

To dos:

Delegated, postponed, declined:

Accomplishments

What, where, when, how, why, who was I today ...

Month _____ Day ___ Year _____

Spiritual: pray, praise, serve ...

Family: love, listen, laugh ...

Friends: reach out, encourage, share ...

Morning rituals: shower, dress, breakfast ...

Vitals: weight, blood pressure, etc.

Medical: medicines, treatments, etc.

Food & nutrition: morning, afternoon, evening (with calories) ...

Exercise: flexibility, cardio, resistance, sports ...

Evening rituals: dinner, family, bed ...

To dos:

Delegated, postponed, declined:

Accomplishments

What, where, when, how, why, who was I today ...

Month _____ Day ___ Year _____

Spiritual: pray, praise, serve ...

Family: love, listen, laugh ...

Friends: reach out, encourage, share ...

Morning rituals: shower, dress, breakfast ...

Vitals: weight, blood pressure, etc.

Medical: medicines, treatments, etc.

Food & nutrition: morning, afternoon, evening (with calories) ...

Exercise: flexibility, cardio, resistance, sports ...

Evening rituals: dinner, family, bed ...

To dos:

Delegated, postponed, declined:

Accomplishments

What, where, when, how, why, who was I today ...

Month _____ Day ___ Year _____

Spiritual: pray, praise, serve ...

Family: love, listen, laugh ...

Friends: reach out, encourage, share ...

Morning rituals: shower, dress, breakfast ...

Vitals: weight, blood pressure, etc.

Medical: medicines, treatments, etc.

Food & nutrition: morning, afternoon, evening (with calories) ...

Exercise: flexibility, cardio, resistance, sports ...

Evening rituals: dinner, family, bed ...

To dos:

Delegated, postponed, declined:

Accomplishments

What, where, when, how, why, who was I today ...

Month _____ Day ___ Year _____

Spiritual: pray, praise, serve ...

Family: love, listen, laugh ...

Friends: reach out, encourage, share ...

Morning rituals: shower, dress, breakfast ...

Vitals: weight, blood pressure, etc.

Medical: medicines, treatments, etc.

Food & nutrition: morning, afternoon, evening (with calories) ...

Exercise: flexibility, cardio, resistance, sports ...

Evening rituals: dinner, family, bed ...

To dos:

Delegated, postponed, declined:

Accomplishments

What, where, when, how, why, who was I today ...

Spiritual: pray, praise, serve ...

Family: love, listen, laugh ...

Friends: reach out, encourage, share ...

Morning rituals: shower, dress, breakfast ...

Vitals: weight, blood pressure, etc.

Medical: medicines, treatments, etc.

Food & nutrition: morning, afternoon, evening (with calories) ...

Exercise: flexibility, cardio, resistance, sports ...

Evening rituals: dinner, family, bed ...

To dos:

Delegated, postponed, declined:

Accomplishments

What, where, when, how, why, who was I today ...

Month _____ Day ___ Year _____

Spiritual: pray, praise, serve ...

Family: love, listen, laugh ...

Friends: reach out, encourage, share ...

Morning rituals: shower, dress, breakfast ...

Vitals: weight, blood pressure, etc.

Medical: medicines, treatments, etc.

Food & nutrition: morning, afternoon, evening (with calories) ...

Exercise: flexibility, cardio, resistance, sports ...

Evening rituals: dinner, family, bed ...

To dos:

Delegated, postponed, declined:

Accomplishments

What, where, when, how, why, who was I today ...

Month _____ Day ___ Year _____

Spiritual: pray, praise, serve ...

Family: love, listen, laugh ...

Friends: reach out, encourage, share ...

Morning rituals: shower, dress, breakfast ...

Vitals: weight, blood pressure, etc.

Medical: medicines, treatments, etc.

Food & nutrition: morning, afternoon, evening (with calories) ...

Exercise: flexibility, cardio, resistance, sports ...

Evening rituals: dinner, family, bed ...

To dos:

Delegated, postponed, declined:

Accomplishments

What, where, when, how, why, who was I today ...

Month _____ Day ___ Year _____

Spiritual: pray, praise, serve ...

Family: love, listen, laugh ...

Friends: reach out, encourage, share ...

Morning rituals: shower, dress, breakfast ...

Vitals: weight, blood pressure, etc.

Medical: medicines, treatments, etc.

Food & nutrition: morning, afternoon, evening (with calories) ...

Exercise: flexibility, cardio, resistance, sports ...

Evening rituals: dinner, family, bed ...

To dos:

Delegated, postponed, declined:

Accomplishments

What, where, when, how, why, who was I today ...

Month _____ Day ___ Year _____

Spiritual: pray, praise, serve ...

Family: love, listen, laugh ...

Friends: reach out, encourage, share ...

Morning rituals: shower, dress, breakfast ...

Vitals: weight, blood pressure, etc.

Medical: medicines, treatments, etc.

Food & nutrition: morning, afternoon, evening (with calories) ...

Exercise: flexibility, cardio, resistance, sports ...

Evening rituals: dinner, family, bed ...

To dos:

Delegated, postponed, declined:

Accomplishments

What, where, when, how, why, who was I today ...

Month _____ Day ___ Year _____

Spiritual: pray, praise, serve ...

Family: love, listen, laugh ...

Friends: reach out, encourage, share ...

Morning rituals: shower, dress, breakfast ...

Vitals: weight, blood pressure, etc.

Medical: medicines, treatments, etc.

Food & nutrition: morning, afternoon, evening (with calories) ...

Exercise: flexibility, cardio, resistance, sports ...

Evening rituals: dinner, family, bed ...

To dos:

Delegated, postponed, declined:

Accomplishments

What, where, when, how, why, who was I today ...

Month _____ Day ___ Year _____

Spiritual: pray, praise, serve ...

Family: love, listen, laugh ...

Friends: reach out, encourage, share ...

Morning rituals: shower, dress, breakfast ...

Vitals: weight, blood pressure, etc.

Medical: medicines, treatments, etc.

Food & nutrition: morning, afternoon, evening (with calories) ...

Exercise: flexibility, cardio, resistance, sports ...

Evening rituals: dinner, family, bed ...

To dos:

Delegated, postponed, declined:

Accomplishments

What, where, when, how, why, who was I today ...

Month _____ Day ___ Year _____

Spiritual: pray, praise, serve ...

Family: love, listen, laugh ...

Friends: reach out, encourage, share ...

Morning rituals: shower, dress, breakfast ...

Vitals: weight, blood pressure, etc.

Medical: medicines, treatments, etc.

Food & nutrition: morning, afternoon, evening (with calories) ...

Exercise: flexibility, cardio, resistance, sports ...

Evening rituals: dinner, family, bed ...

To dos:

Delegated, postponed, declined:

Accomplishments

What, where, when, how, why, who was I today ...

Month _____ Day ___ Year _____

Spiritual: pray, praise, serve ...

Family: love, listen, laugh ...

Friends: reach out, encourage, share ...

Morning rituals: shower, dress, breakfast ...

Vitals: weight, blood pressure, etc.

Medical: medicines, treatments, etc.

Food & nutrition: morning, afternoon, evening (with calories) ...

Exercise: flexibility, cardio, resistance, sports ...

Evening rituals: dinner, family, bed ...

To dos:

Delegated, postponed, declined:

Accomplishments

What, where, when, how, why, who was I today ...

Month _____ Day ___ Year _____

Spiritual: pray, praise, serve ...

Family: love, listen, laugh ...

Friends: reach out, encourage, share ...

Morning rituals: shower, dress, breakfast ...

Vitals: weight, blood pressure, etc.

Medical: medicines, treatments, etc.

Food & nutrition: morning, afternoon, evening (with calories) ...

Exercise: flexibility, cardio, resistance, sports ...

Evening rituals: dinner, family, bed ...

To dos:

Delegated, postponed, declined:

Accomplishments

What, where, when, how, why, who was I today ...

Month _____ Day ___ Year _____

Spiritual: pray, praise, serve ...

Family: love, listen, laugh ...

Friends: reach out, encourage, share ...

Morning rituals: shower, dress, breakfast ...

Vitals: weight, blood pressure, etc.

Medical: medicines, treatments, etc.

Food & nutrition: morning, afternoon, evening (with calories) ...

Exercise: flexibility, cardio, resistance, sports ...

Evening rituals: dinner, family, bed ...

To dos:

Delegated, postponed, declined:

Accomplishments

What, where, when, how, why, who was I today ...

Month _____ Day ___ Year _____

Spiritual: pray, praise, serve ...

Family: love, listen, laugh ...

Friends: reach out, encourage, share ...

Morning rituals: shower, dress, breakfast ...

Vitals: weight, blood pressure, etc.

Medical: medicines, treatments, etc.

Food & nutrition: morning, afternoon, evening (with calories) ...

Exercise: flexibility, cardio, resistance, sports ...

Evening rituals: dinner, family, bed ...

To dos:

Delegated, postponed, declined:

Accomplishments

What, where, when, how, why, who was I today ...

Spiritual: pray, praise, serve ...

Family: love, listen, laugh ...

Friends: reach out, encourage, share ...

Morning rituals: shower, dress, breakfast ...

Vitals: weight, blood pressure, etc.

Medical: medicines, treatments, etc.

Food & nutrition: morning, afternoon, evening (with calories) ...

Exercise: flexibility, cardio, resistance, sports ...

Evening rituals: dinner, family, bed ...

To dos:

Delegated, postponed, declined:

Accomplishments

What, where, when, how, why, who was I today ...

Month _____ Day ___ Year _____

Spiritual: pray, praise, serve ...

Family: love, listen, laugh ...

Friends: reach out, encourage, share ...

Morning rituals: shower, dress, breakfast ...

Vitals: weight, blood pressure, etc.

Medical: medicines, treatments, etc.

Food & nutrition: morning, afternoon, evening (with calories) ...

Exercise: flexibility, cardio, resistance, sports ...

Evening rituals: dinner, family, bed ...

To dos:

Delegated, postponed, declined:

Accomplishments

What, where, when, how, why, who was I today ...

Spiritual: pray, praise, serve ...

Family: love, listen, laugh ...

Friends: reach out, encourage, share ...

Morning rituals: shower, dress, breakfast ...

Vitals: weight, blood pressure, etc.

Medical: medicines, treatments, etc.

Food & nutrition: morning, afternoon, evening (with calories) ...

Exercise: flexibility, cardio, resistance, sports ...

Evening rituals: dinner, family, bed ...

To dos:

Delegated, postponed, declined:

Accomplishments

What, where, when, how, why, who was I today ...

Month _____ Day ___ Year _____

Spiritual: pray, praise, serve ...

Family: love, listen, laugh ...

Friends: reach out, encourage, share ...

Morning rituals: shower, dress, breakfast ...

Vitals: weight, blood pressure, etc.

Medical: medicines, treatments, etc.

Food & nutrition: morning, afternoon, evening (with calories) ...

Exercise: flexibility, cardio, resistance, sports ...

Evening rituals: dinner, family, bed ...

To dos:

Delegated, postponed, declined:

Accomplishments

What, where, when, how, why, who was I today ...

Spiritual: pray, praise, serve ...

Family: love, listen, laugh ...

Friends: reach out, encourage, share ...

Morning rituals: shower, dress, breakfast ...

Vitals: weight, blood pressure, etc.

Medical: medicines, treatments, etc.

Food & nutrition: morning, afternoon, evening (with calories) ...

Exercise: flexibility, cardio, resistance, sports ...

Evening rituals: dinner, family, bed ...

To dos:

Delegated, postponed, declined:

Accomplishments

What, where, when, how, why, who was I today ...

Month _____ Day ____ Year _____

Spiritual: pray, praise, serve ...

Family: love, listen, laugh ...

Friends: reach out, encourage, share ...

Morning rituals: shower, dress, breakfast ...

Vitals: weight, blood pressure, etc.

Medical: medicines, treatments, etc.

Food & nutrition: morning, afternoon, evening (with calories) ...

Exercise: flexibility, cardio, resistance, sports ...

Evening rituals: dinner, family, bed ...

To dos:

Delegated, postponed, declined:

Accomplishments

What, where, when, how, why, who was I today ...

Spiritual: pray, praise, serve ...

Family: love, listen, laugh ...

Friends: reach out, encourage, share ...

Morning rituals: shower, dress, breakfast ...

Vitals: weight, blood pressure, etc.

Medical: medicines, treatments, etc.

Food & nutrition: morning, afternoon, evening (with calories) ...

Exercise: flexibility, cardio, resistance, sports ...

Evening rituals: dinner, family, bed ...

To dos:

Delegated, postponed, declined:

Accomplishments

What, where, when, how, why, who was I today ...

Month _____ Day ____ Year _____

Spiritual: pray, praise, serve ...

Family: love, listen, laugh ...

Friends: reach out, encourage, share ...

Morning rituals: shower, dress, breakfast ...

Vitals: weight, blood pressure, etc.

Medical: medicines, treatments, etc.

Food & nutrition: morning, afternoon, evening (with calories) ...

Exercise: flexibility, cardio, resistance, sports ...

Evening rituals: dinner, family, bed ...

To dos:

Delegated, postponed, declined:

Accomplishments

What, where, when, how, why, who was I today ...

Month _____ Day ___ Year _____

Spiritual: pray, praise, serve ...

Family: love, listen, laugh ...

Friends: reach out, encourage, share ...

Morning rituals: shower, dress, breakfast ...

Vitals: weight, blood pressure, etc.

Medical: medicines, treatments, etc.

Food & nutrition: morning, afternoon, evening (with calories) ...

Exercise: flexibility, cardio, resistance, sports ...

Evening rituals: dinner, family, bed ...

To dos:

Delegated, postponed, declined:

Accomplishments

What, where, when, how, why, who was I today ...

Month _____ Day ___ Year _____

Spiritual: pray, praise, serve ...

Family: love, listen, laugh ...

Friends: reach out, encourage, share ...

Morning rituals: shower, dress, breakfast ...

Vitals: weight, blood pressure, etc.

Medical: medicines, treatments, etc.

Food & nutrition: morning, afternoon, evening (with calories) ...

Exercise: flexibility, cardio, resistance, sports ...

Evening rituals: dinner, family, bed ...

To dos:

Delegated, postponed, declined:

Accomplishments

What, where, when, how, why, who was I today ...

Month _____ Day ____ Year _____

Spiritual: pray, praise, serve ...

Family: love, listen, laugh ...

Friends: reach out, encourage, share ...

Morning rituals: shower, dress, breakfast ...

Vitals: weight, blood pressure, etc.

Medical: medicines, treatments, etc.

Food & nutrition: morning, afternoon, evening (with calories) ...

Exercise: flexibility, cardio, resistance, sports ...

Evening rituals: dinner, family, bed ...

To dos:

Delegated, postponed, declined:

Accomplishments

What, where, when, how, why, who was I today ...

Month _____ Day ___ Year _____

Spiritual: pray, praise, serve ...

Family: love, listen, laugh ...

Friends: reach out, encourage, share ...

Morning rituals: shower, dress, breakfast ...

Vitals: weight, blood pressure, etc.

Medical: medicines, treatments, etc.

Food & nutrition: morning, afternoon, evening (with calories) ...

Exercise: flexibility, cardio, resistance, sports ...

Evening rituals: dinner, family, bed ...

To dos:

Delegated, postponed, declined:

Accomplishments

What, where, when, how, why, who was I today ...

Month _____ Day ____ Year _____

Spiritual: pray, praise, serve ...

Family: love, listen, laugh ...

Friends: reach out, encourage, share ...

Morning rituals: shower, dress, breakfast ...

Vitals: weight, blood pressure, etc.

Medical: medicines, treatments, etc.

Food & nutrition: morning, afternoon, evening (with calories) ...

Exercise: flexibility, cardio, resistance, sports ...

Evening rituals: dinner, family, bed ...

To dos:

Delegated, postponed, declined:

Accomplishments

What, where, when, how, why, who was I today ...

Month _____ Day ___ Year _____

Spiritual: pray, praise, serve ...

Family: love, listen, laugh ...

Friends: reach out, encourage, share ...

Morning rituals: shower, dress, breakfast ...

Vitals: weight, blood pressure, etc.

Medical: medicines, treatments, etc.

Food & nutrition: morning, afternoon, evening (with calories) ...

Exercise: flexibility, cardio, resistance, sports ...

Evening rituals: dinner, family, bed ...

To dos:

Delegated, postponed, declined:

Accomplishments

What, where, when, how, why, who was I today ...

Spiritual: pray, praise, serve ...

Family: love, listen, laugh ...

Friends: reach out, encourage, share ...

Morning rituals: shower, dress, breakfast ...

Vitals: weight, blood pressure, etc.

Medical: medicines, treatments, etc.

Food & nutrition: morning, afternoon, evening (with calories) ...

Exercise: flexibility, cardio, resistance, sports ...

Evening rituals: dinner, family, bed ...

To dos:

Delegated, postponed, declined:

Accomplishments

What, where, when, how, why, who was I today ...

Month _____ Day ___ Year _____

Spiritual: pray, praise, serve ...

Family: love, listen, laugh ...

Friends: reach out, encourage, share ...

Morning rituals: shower, dress, breakfast ...

Vitals: weight, blood pressure, etc.

Medical: medicines, treatments, etc.

Food & nutrition: morning, afternoon, evening (with calories) ...

Exercise: flexibility, cardio, resistance, sports ...

Evening rituals: dinner, family, bed ...

To dos:

Delegated, postponed, declined:

Accomplishments

What, where, when, how, why, who was I today ...

Spiritual: pray, praise, serve ...

Family: love, listen, laugh ...

Friends: reach out, encourage, share ...

Morning rituals: shower, dress, breakfast ...

Vitals: weight, blood pressure, etc.

Medical: medicines, treatments, etc.

Food & nutrition: morning, afternoon, evening (with calories) ...

Exercise: flexibility, cardio, resistance, sports ...

Evening rituals: dinner, family, bed ...

To dos:

Delegated, postponed, declined:

Accomplishments

What, where, when, how, why, who was I today ...

Month _____ Day ___ Year _____

Spiritual: pray, praise, serve ...

Family: love, listen, laugh ...

Friends: reach out, encourage, share ...

Morning rituals: shower, dress, breakfast ...

Vitals: weight, blood pressure, etc.

Medical: medicines, treatments, etc.

Food & nutrition: morning, afternoon, evening (with calories) ...

Exercise: flexibility, cardio, resistance, sports ...

Evening rituals: dinner, family, bed ...

To dos:

Delegated, postponed, declined:

Accomplishments

What, where, when, how, why, who was I today ...

Spiritual: pray, praise, serve ...

Family: love, listen, laugh ...

Friends: reach out, encourage, share ...

Morning rituals: shower, dress, breakfast ...

Vitals: weight, blood pressure, etc.

Medical: medicines, treatments, etc.

Food & nutrition: morning, afternoon, evening (with calories) ...

Exercise: flexibility, cardio, resistance, sports ...

Evening rituals: dinner, family, bed ...

To dos:

Delegated, postponed, declined:

Accomplishments

What, where, when, how, why, who was I today ...

Month _____ Day ___ Year _____

Spiritual: pray, praise, serve ...

Family: love, listen, laugh ...

Friends: reach out, encourage, share ...

Morning rituals: shower, dress, breakfast ...

Vitals: weight, blood pressure, etc.

Medical: medicines, treatments, etc.

Food & nutrition: morning, afternoon, evening (with calories) ...

Exercise: flexibility, cardio, resistance, sports ...

Evening rituals: dinner, family, bed ...

To dos:

Delegated, postponed, declined:

Accomplishments

What, where, when, how, why, who was I today ...

Spiritual: pray, praise, serve ...

Family: love, listen, laugh ...

Friends: reach out, encourage, share ...

Morning rituals: shower, dress, breakfast ...

Vitals: weight, blood pressure, etc.

Medical: medicines, treatments, etc.

Food & nutrition: morning, afternoon, evening (with calories) ...

Exercise: flexibility, cardio, resistance, sports ...

Evening rituals: dinner, family, bed ...

To dos:

Delegated, postponed, declined:

Accomplishments

What, where, when, how, why, who was I today ...

Month _____ Day ___ Year _____

Spiritual: pray, praise, serve ...

Family: love, listen, laugh ...

Friends: reach out, encourage, share ...

Morning rituals: shower, dress, breakfast ...

Vitals: weight, blood pressure, etc.

Medical: medicines, treatments, etc.

Food & nutrition: morning, afternoon, evening (with calories) ...

Exercise: flexibility, cardio, resistance, sports ...

Evening rituals: dinner, family, bed ...

To dos:

Delegated, postponed, declined:

Accomplishments

What, where, when, how, why, who was I today ...

Month _____ Day ___ Year _____

Spiritual: pray, praise, serve ...

Family: love, listen, laugh ...

Friends: reach out, encourage, share ...

Morning rituals: shower, dress, breakfast ...

Vitals: weight, blood pressure, etc.

Medical: medicines, treatments, etc.

Food & nutrition: morning, afternoon, evening (with calories) ...

Exercise: flexibility, cardio, resistance, sports ...

Evening rituals: dinner, family, bed ...

To dos:

Delegated, postponed, declined:

Accomplishments

What, where, when, how, why, who was I today ...

Month _____ Day ___ Year _____

Spiritual: pray, praise, serve ...

Family: love, listen, laugh ...

Friends: reach out, encourage, share ...

Morning rituals: shower, dress, breakfast ...

Vitals: weight, blood pressure, etc.

Medical: medicines, treatments, etc.

Food & nutrition: morning, afternoon, evening (with calories) ...

Exercise: flexibility, cardio, resistance, sports ...

Evening rituals: dinner, family, bed ...

To dos:

Delegated, postponed, declined:

Accomplishments

What, where, when, how, why, who was I today ...

Month _____ Day ___ Year _____

Spiritual: pray, praise, serve ...

Family: love, listen, laugh ...

Friends: reach out, encourage, share ...

Morning rituals: shower, dress, breakfast ...

Vitals: weight, blood pressure, etc.

Medical: medicines, treatments, etc.

Food & nutrition: morning, afternoon, evening (with calories) ...

Exercise: flexibility, cardio, resistance, sports ...

Evening rituals: dinner, family, bed ...

To dos:

Delegated, postponed, declined:

Accomplishments

What, where, when, how, why, who was I today ...

Month _____ Day ____ Year _____

Spiritual: pray, praise, serve ...

Family: love, listen, laugh ...

Friends: reach out, encourage, share ...

Morning rituals: shower, dress, breakfast ...

Vitals: weight, blood pressure, etc.

Medical: medicines, treatments, etc.

Food & nutrition: morning, afternoon, evening (with calories) ...

Exercise: flexibility, cardio, resistance, sports ...

Evening rituals: dinner, family, bed ...

To dos:

Delegated, postponed, declined:

Accomplishments

What, where, when, how, why, who was I today ...

Month _____ Day ___ Year _____

Spiritual: pray, praise, serve ...

Family: love, listen, laugh ...

Friends: reach out, encourage, share ...

Morning rituals: shower, dress, breakfast ...

Vitals: weight, blood pressure, etc.

Medical: medicines, treatments, etc.

Food & nutrition: morning, afternoon, evening (with calories) ...

Exercise: flexibility, cardio, resistance, sports ...

Evening rituals: dinner, family, bed ...

To dos:

Delegated, postponed, declined:

Accomplishments

What, where, when, how, why, who was I today ...

Month _____ Day ___ Year _____

Spiritual: pray, praise, serve ...

Family: love, listen, laugh ...

Friends: reach out, encourage, share ...

Morning rituals: shower, dress, breakfast ...

Vitals: weight, blood pressure, etc.

Medical: medicines, treatments, etc.

Food & nutrition: morning, afternoon, evening (with calories) ...

Exercise: flexibility, cardio, resistance, sports ...

Evening rituals: dinner, family, bed ...

To dos:

Delegated, postponed, declined:

Accomplishments

What, where, when, how, why, who was I today ...

Spiritual: pray, praise, serve ...

Family: love, listen, laugh ...

Friends: reach out, encourage, share ...

Morning rituals: shower, dress, breakfast ...

Vitals: weight, blood pressure, etc.

Medical: medicines, treatments, etc.

Food & nutrition: morning, afternoon, evening (with calories) ...

Exercise: flexibility, cardio, resistance, sports ...

Evening rituals: dinner, family, bed ...

To dos:

Delegated, postponed, declined:

Accomplishments

What, where, when, how, why, who was I today ...

Month _____ Day ____ Year _____

Spiritual: pray, praise, serve ...

Family: love, listen, laugh ...

Friends: reach out, encourage, share ...

Morning rituals: shower, dress, breakfast ...

Vitals: weight, blood pressure, etc.

Medical: medicines, treatments, etc.

Food & nutrition: morning, afternoon, evening (with calories) ...

Exercise: flexibility, cardio, resistance, sports ...

Evening rituals: dinner, family, bed ...

To dos:

Delegated, postponed, declined:

Accomplishments

What, where, when, how, why, who was I today ...

Month _____ Day ___ Year _____

Spiritual: pray, praise, serve ...

Family: love, listen, laugh ...

Friends: reach out, encourage, share ...

Morning rituals: shower, dress, breakfast ...

Vitals: weight, blood pressure, etc.

Medical: medicines, treatments, etc.

Food & nutrition: morning, afternoon, evening (with calories) ...

Exercise: flexibility, cardio, resistance, sports ...

Evening rituals: dinner, family, bed ...

To dos:

Delegated, postponed, declined:

Accomplishments

What, where, when, how, why, who was I today ...

Month _____ Day ___ Year _____

Spiritual: pray, praise, serve ...

Family: love, listen, laugh ...

Friends: reach out, encourage, share ...

Morning rituals: shower, dress, breakfast ...

Vitals: weight, blood pressure, etc.

Medical: medicines, treatments, etc.

Food & nutrition: morning, afternoon, evening (with calories) ...

Exercise: flexibility, cardio, resistance, sports ...

Evening rituals: dinner, family, bed ...

To dos:

Delegated, postponed, declined:

Accomplishments

What, where, when, how, why, who was I today ...

Month _____ Day ___ Year _____

Spiritual: pray, praise, serve ...

Family: love, listen, laugh ...

Friends: reach out, encourage, share ...

Morning rituals: shower, dress, breakfast ...

Vitals: weight, blood pressure, etc.

Medical: medicines, treatments, etc.

Food & nutrition: morning, afternoon, evening (with calories) ...

Exercise: flexibility, cardio, resistance, sports ...

Evening rituals: dinner, family, bed ...

To dos:

Delegated, postponed, declined:

Accomplishments

What, where, when, how, why, who was I today ...

Month _____ Day ___ Year _____

Spiritual: pray, praise, serve ...

Family: love, listen, laugh ...

Friends: reach out, encourage, share ...

Morning rituals: shower, dress, breakfast ...

Vitals: weight, blood pressure, etc.

Medical: medicines, treatments, etc.

Food & nutrition: morning, afternoon, evening (with calories) ...

Exercise: flexibility, cardio, resistance, sports ...

Evening rituals: dinner, family, bed ...

To dos:

Delegated, postponed, declined:

Accomplishments

What, where, when, how, why, who was I today ...

Month _____ Day ___ Year _____

Spiritual: pray, praise, serve ...

Family: love, listen, laugh ...

Friends: reach out, encourage, share ...

Morning rituals: shower, dress, breakfast ...

Vitals: weight, blood pressure, etc.

Medical: medicines, treatments, etc.

Food & nutrition: morning, afternoon, evening (with calories) ...

Exercise: flexibility, cardio, resistance, sports ...

Evening rituals: dinner, family, bed ...

To dos:

Delegated, postponed, declined:

Accomplishments

What, where, when, how, why, who was I today ...

Month _____ Day ___ Year _____

Spiritual: pray, praise, serve ...

Family: love, listen, laugh ...

Friends: reach out, encourage, share ...

Morning rituals: shower, dress, breakfast ...

Vitals: weight, blood pressure, etc.

Medical: medicines, treatments, etc.

Food & nutrition: morning, afternoon, evening (with calories) ...

Exercise: flexibility, cardio, resistance, sports ...

Evening rituals: dinner, family, bed ...

To dos:

Delegated, postponed, declined:

Accomplishments

What, where, when, how, why, who was I today ...

Month _____ Day ___ Year _____

Spiritual: pray, praise, serve ...

Family: love, listen, laugh ...

Friends: reach out, encourage, share ...

Morning rituals: shower, dress, breakfast ...

Vitals: weight, blood pressure, etc.

Medical: medicines, treatments, etc.

Food & nutrition: morning, afternoon, evening (with calories) ...

Exercise: flexibility, cardio, resistance, sports ...

Evening rituals: dinner, family, bed ...

To dos:

Delegated, postponed, declined:

Accomplishments

What, where, when, how, why, who was I today ...

Month _____ Day ___ Year _____

Spiritual: pray, praise, serve ...

Family: love, listen, laugh ...

Friends: reach out, encourage, share ...

Morning rituals: shower, dress, breakfast ...

Vitals: weight, blood pressure, etc.

Medical: medicines, treatments, etc.

Food & nutrition: morning, afternoon, evening (with calories) ...

Exercise: flexibility, cardio, resistance, sports ...

Evening rituals: dinner, family, bed ...

To dos:

Delegated, postponed, declined:

Accomplishments

What, where, when, how, why, who was I today ...

Month _____ Day ___ Year _____

Spiritual: pray, praise, serve ...

Family: love, listen, laugh ...

Friends: reach out, encourage, share ...

Morning rituals: shower, dress, breakfast ...

Vitals: weight, blood pressure, etc.

Medical: medicines, treatments, etc.

Food & nutrition: morning, afternoon, evening (with calories) ...

Exercise: flexibility, cardio, resistance, sports ...

Evening rituals: dinner, family, bed ...

To dos:

Delegated, postponed, declined:

Accomplishments

What, where, when, how, why, who was I today ...

Month _____ Day ___ Year _____

Spiritual: pray, praise, serve ...

Family: love, listen, laugh ...

Friends: reach out, encourage, share ...

Morning rituals: shower, dress, breakfast ...

Vitals: weight, blood pressure, etc.

Medical: medicines, treatments, etc.

Food & nutrition: morning, afternoon, evening (with calories) ...

Exercise: flexibility, cardio, resistance, sports ...

Evening rituals: dinner, family, bed ...

To dos:

Delegated, postponed, declined:

Accomplishments

What, where, when, how, why, who was I today ...

Month _____ Day ___ Year _____

Spiritual: pray, praise, serve ...

Family: love, listen, laugh ...

Friends: reach out, encourage, share ...

Morning rituals: shower, dress, breakfast ...

Vitals: weight, blood pressure, etc.

Medical: medicines, treatments, etc.

Food & nutrition: morning, afternoon, evening (with calories) ...

Exercise: flexibility, cardio, resistance, sports ...

Evening rituals: dinner, family, bed ...

To dos:

Delegated, postponed, declined:

Accomplishments

What, where, when, how, why, who was I today ...

Month _____ Day ___ Year _____

Spiritual: pray, praise, serve ...

Family: love, listen, laugh ...

Friends: reach out, encourage, share ...

Morning rituals: shower, dress, breakfast ...

Vitals: weight, blood pressure, etc.

Medical: medicines, treatments, etc.

Food & nutrition: morning, afternoon, evening (with calories) ...

Exercise: flexibility, cardio, resistance, sports ...

Evening rituals: dinner, family, bed ...

To dos:

Delegated, postponed, declined:

Accomplishments

What, where, when, how, why, who was I today ...

Month _____ Day ___ Year _____

Spiritual: pray, praise, serve ...

Family: love, listen, laugh ...

Friends: reach out, encourage, share ...

Morning rituals: shower, dress, breakfast ...

Vitals: weight, blood pressure, etc.

Medical: medicines, treatments, etc.

Food & nutrition: morning, afternoon, evening (with calories) ...

Exercise: flexibility, cardio, resistance, sports ...

Evening rituals: dinner, family, bed ...

To dos:

Delegated, postponed, declined:

Accomplishments

What, where, when, how, why, who was I today ...

Month _____ Day ___ Year _____

Spiritual: pray, praise, serve ...

Family: love, listen, laugh ...

Friends: reach out, encourage, share ...

Morning rituals: shower, dress, breakfast ...

Vitals: weight, blood pressure, etc.

Medical: medicines, treatments, etc.

Food & nutrition: morning, afternoon, evening (with calories) ...

Exercise: flexibility, cardio, resistance, sports ...

Evening rituals: dinner, family, bed ...

To dos:

Delegated, postponed, declined:

Accomplishments

What, where, when, how, why, who was I today ...

Month _____ Day ____ Year _____

Spiritual: pray, praise, serve ...

Family: love, listen, laugh ...

Friends: reach out, encourage, share ...

Morning rituals: shower, dress, breakfast ...

Vitals: weight, blood pressure, etc.

Medical: medicines, treatments, etc.

Food & nutrition: morning, afternoon, evening (with calories) ...

Exercise: flexibility, cardio, resistance, sports ...

Evening rituals: dinner, family, bed ...

To dos:

Delegated, postponed, declined:

Accomplishments

What, where, when, how, why, who was I today ...

Month _____ Day ___ Year _____

Spiritual: pray, praise, serve ...

Family: love, listen, laugh ...

Friends: reach out, encourage, share ...

Morning rituals: shower, dress, breakfast ...

Vitals: weight, blood pressure, etc.

Medical: medicines, treatments, etc.

Food & nutrition: morning, afternoon, evening (with calories) ...

Exercise: flexibility, cardio, resistance, sports ...

Evening rituals: dinner, family, bed ...

To dos:

Delegated, postponed, declined:

Accomplishments

What, where, when, how, why, who was I today ...

Month _____ Day ___ Year _____

Spiritual: pray, praise, serve ...

Family: love, listen, laugh ...

Friends: reach out, encourage, share ...

Morning rituals: shower, dress, breakfast ...

Vitals: weight, blood pressure, etc.

Medical: medicines, treatments, etc.

Food & nutrition: morning, afternoon, evening (with calories) ...

Exercise: flexibility, cardio, resistance, sports ...

Evening rituals: dinner, family, bed ...

To dos:

Delegated, postponed, declined:

Accomplishments

What, where, when, how, why, who was I today ...

Month _____ Day ___ Year _____

Spiritual: pray, praise, serve ...

Family: love, listen, laugh ...

Friends: reach out, encourage, share ...

Morning rituals: shower, dress, breakfast ...

Vitals: weight, blood pressure, etc.

Medical: medicines, treatments, etc.

Food & nutrition: morning, afternoon, evening (with calories) ...

Exercise: flexibility, cardio, resistance, sports ...

Evening rituals: dinner, family, bed ...

To dos:

Delegated, postponed, declined:

Accomplishments

What, where, when, how, why, who was I today ...

Month _____ Day ___ Year _____

Spiritual: pray, praise, serve ...

Family: love, listen, laugh ...

Friends: reach out, encourage, share ...

Morning rituals: shower, dress, breakfast ...

Vitals: weight, blood pressure, etc.

Medical: medicines, treatments, etc.

Food & nutrition: morning, afternoon, evening (with calories) ...

Exercise: flexibility, cardio, resistance, sports ...

Evening rituals: dinner, family, bed ...

To dos:

Delegated, postponed, declined:

Accomplishments

What, where, when, how, why, who was I today ...

Month _____ Day ___ Year _____

Spiritual: pray, praise, serve ...

Family: love, listen, laugh ...

Friends: reach out, encourage, share ...

Morning rituals: shower, dress, breakfast ...

Vitals: weight, blood pressure, etc.

Medical: medicines, treatments, etc.

Food & nutrition: morning, afternoon, evening (with calories) ...

Exercise: flexibility, cardio, resistance, sports ...

Evening rituals: dinner, family, bed ...

To dos:

Delegated, postponed, declined:

Accomplishments

What, where, when, how, why, who was I today ...

Spiritual: pray, praise, serve ...

Family: love, listen, laugh ...

Friends: reach out, encourage, share ...

Morning rituals: shower, dress, breakfast ...

Vitals: weight, blood pressure, etc.

Medical: medicines, treatments, etc.

Food & nutrition: morning, afternoon, evening (with calories) ...

Exercise: flexibility, cardio, resistance, sports ...

Evening rituals: dinner, family, bed ...

To dos:

Delegated, postponed, declined:

Accomplishments

What, where, when, how, why, who was I today ...

Month _____ Day ___ Year _____

Spiritual: pray, praise, serve ...

Family: love, listen, laugh ...

Friends: reach out, encourage, share ...

Morning rituals: shower, dress, breakfast ...

Vitals: weight, blood pressure, etc.

Medical: medicines, treatments, etc.

Food & nutrition: morning, afternoon, evening (with calories) ...

Exercise: flexibility, cardio, resistance, sports ...

Evening rituals: dinner, family, bed ...

To dos:

Delegated, postponed, declined:

Accomplishments

What, where, when, how, why, who was I today ...

Month _____ Day ___ Year _____

Spiritual: pray, praise, serve ...

Family: love, listen, laugh ...

Friends: reach out, encourage, share ...

Morning rituals: shower, dress, breakfast ...

Vitals: weight, blood pressure, etc.

Medical: medicines, treatments, etc.

Food & nutrition: morning, afternoon, evening (with calories) ...

Exercise: flexibility, cardio, resistance, sports ...

Evening rituals: dinner, family, bed ...

To dos:

Delegated, postponed, declined:

Accomplishments

What, where, when, how, why, who was I today ...

Month _____ Day ___ Year _____

Spiritual: pray, praise, serve ...

Family: love, listen, laugh ...

Friends: reach out, encourage, share ...

Morning rituals: shower, dress, breakfast ...

Vitals: weight, blood pressure, etc.

Medical: medicines, treatments, etc.

Food & nutrition: morning, afternoon, evening (with calories) ...

Exercise: flexibility, cardio, resistance, sports ...

Evening rituals: dinner, family, bed ...

To dos:

Delegated, postponed, declined:

Accomplishments

What, where, when, how, why, who was I today ...

Month _____ Day ___ Year _____

Spiritual: pray, praise, serve ...

Family: love, listen, laugh ...

Friends: reach out, encourage, share ...

Morning rituals: shower, dress, breakfast ...

Vitals: weight, blood pressure, etc.

Medical: medicines, treatments, etc.

Food & nutrition: morning, afternoon, evening (with calories) ...

Exercise: flexibility, cardio, resistance, sports ...

Evening rituals: dinner, family, bed ...

To dos:

Delegated, postponed, declined:

Accomplishments

What, where, when, how, why, who was I today ...

Month _____ Day ___ Year _____

Spiritual: pray, praise, serve ...

Family: love, listen, laugh ...

Friends: reach out, encourage, share ...

Morning rituals: shower, dress, breakfast ...

Vitals: weight, blood pressure, etc.

Medical: medicines, treatments, etc.

Food & nutrition: morning, afternoon, evening (with calories) ...

Exercise: flexibility, cardio, resistance, sports ...

Evening rituals: dinner, family, bed ...

To dos:

Delegated, postponed, declined:

Accomplishments

What, where, when, how, why, who was I today ...

Month _____ Day ___ Year _____

Spiritual: pray, praise, serve ...

Family: love, listen, laugh ...

Friends: reach out, encourage, share ...

Morning rituals: shower, dress, breakfast ...

Vitals: weight, blood pressure, etc.

Medical: medicines, treatments, etc.

Food & nutrition: morning, afternoon, evening (with calories) ...

Exercise: flexibility, cardio, resistance, sports ...

Evening rituals: dinner, family, bed ...

To dos:

Delegated, postponed, declined:

Accomplishments

What, where, when, how, why, who was I today ...

Month _____ Day ___ Year _____

Spiritual: pray, praise, serve ...

Family: love, listen, laugh ...

Friends: reach out, encourage, share ...

Morning rituals: shower, dress, breakfast ...

Vitals: weight, blood pressure, etc.

Medical: medicines, treatments, etc.

Food & nutrition: morning, afternoon, evening (with calories) ...

Exercise: flexibility, cardio, resistance, sports ...

Evening rituals: dinner, family, bed ...

To dos:

Delegated, postponed, declined:

Accomplishments

What, where, when, how, why, who was I today ...

Month _____ Day ___ Year _____

Spiritual: pray, praise, serve ...

Family: love, listen, laugh ...

Friends: reach out, encourage, share ...

Morning rituals: shower, dress, breakfast ...

Vitals: weight, blood pressure, etc.

Medical: medicines, treatments, etc.

Food & nutrition: morning, afternoon, evening (with calories) ...

Exercise: flexibility, cardio, resistance, sports ...

Evening rituals: dinner, family, bed ...

To dos:

Delegated, postponed, declined:

Accomplishments

What, where, when, how, why, who was I today ...

Month _____ Day ___ Year _____

Spiritual: pray, praise, serve ...

Family: love, listen, laugh ...

Friends: reach out, encourage, share ...

Morning rituals: shower, dress, breakfast ...

Vitals: weight, blood pressure, etc.

Medical: medicines, treatments, etc.

Food & nutrition: morning, afternoon, evening (with calories) ...

Exercise: flexibility, cardio, resistance, sports ...

Evening rituals: dinner, family, bed ...

To dos:

Delegated, postponed, declined:

Accomplishments

What, where, when, how, why, who was I today ...

Month _____ Day ___ Year _____

Spiritual: pray, praise, serve ...

Family: love, listen, laugh ...

Friends: reach out, encourage, share ...

Morning rituals: shower, dress, breakfast ...

Vitals: weight, blood pressure, etc.

Medical: medicines, treatments, etc.

Food & nutrition: morning, afternoon, evening (with calories) ...

Exercise: flexibility, cardio, resistance, sports ...

Evening rituals: dinner, family, bed ...

To dos:

Delegated, postponed, declined:

Accomplishments

What, where, when, how, why, who was I today ...

Month _____ Day ___ Year _____

Spiritual: pray, praise, serve ...

Family: love, listen, laugh ...

Friends: reach out, encourage, share ...

Morning rituals: shower, dress, breakfast ...

Vitals: weight, blood pressure, etc.

Medical: medicines, treatments, etc.

Food & nutrition: morning, afternoon, evening (with calories) ...

Exercise: flexibility, cardio, resistance, sports ...

Evening rituals: dinner, family, bed ...

To dos:

Delegated, postponed, declined:

Accomplishments

What, where, when, how, why, who was I today ...

Month _____ Day ___ Year _____

Spiritual: pray, praise, serve ...

Family: love, listen, laugh ...

Friends: reach out, encourage, share ...

Morning rituals: shower, dress, breakfast ...

Vitals: weight, blood pressure, etc.

Medical: medicines, treatments, etc.

Food & nutrition: morning, afternoon, evening (with calories) ...

Exercise: flexibility, cardio, resistance, sports ...

Evening rituals: dinner, family, bed ...

To dos:

Delegated, postponed, declined:

Accomplishments

What, where, when, how, why, who was I today ...

Month _____ Day ___ Year _____

Spiritual: pray, praise, serve ...

Family: love, listen, laugh ...

Friends: reach out, encourage, share ...

Morning rituals: shower, dress, breakfast ...

Vitals: weight, blood pressure, etc.

Medical: medicines, treatments, etc.

Food & nutrition: morning, afternoon, evening (with calories) ...

Exercise: flexibility, cardio, resistance, sports ...

Evening rituals: dinner, family, bed ...

To dos:

Delegated, postponed, declined:

Accomplishments

What, where, when, how, why, who was I today ...

Spiritual: pray, praise, serve ...

Family: love, listen, laugh ...

Friends: reach out, encourage, share ...

Morning rituals: shower, dress, breakfast ...

Vitals: weight, blood pressure, etc.

Medical: medicines, treatments, etc.

Food & nutrition: morning, afternoon, evening (with calories) ...

Exercise: flexibility, cardio, resistance, sports ...

Evening rituals: dinner, family, bed ...

To dos:

Delegated, postponed, declined:

Accomplishments

What, where, when, how, why, who was I today ...

Month _____ Day ___ Year _____

Spiritual: pray, praise, serve ...

Family: love, listen, laugh ...

Friends: reach out, encourage, share ...

Morning rituals: shower, dress, breakfast ...

Vitals: weight, blood pressure, etc.

Medical: medicines, treatments, etc.

Food & nutrition: morning, afternoon, evening (with calories) ...

Exercise: flexibility, cardio, resistance, sports ...

Evening rituals: dinner, family, bed ...

To dos:

Delegated, postponed, declined:

Accomplishments

What, where, when, how, why, who was I today ...

Month _____ Day ___ Year _____

Spiritual: pray, praise, serve ...

Family: love, listen, laugh ...

Friends: reach out, encourage, share ...

Morning rituals: shower, dress, breakfast ...

Vitals: weight, blood pressure, etc.

Medical: medicines, treatments, etc.

Food & nutrition: morning, afternoon, evening (with calories) ...

Exercise: flexibility, cardio, resistance, sports ...

Evening rituals: dinner, family, bed ...

To dos:

Delegated, postponed, declined:

Accomplishments

What, where, when, how, why, who was I today ...

Month _____ Day ___ Year _____

Spiritual: pray, praise, serve ...

Family: love, listen, laugh ...

Friends: reach out, encourage, share ...

Morning rituals: shower, dress, breakfast ...

Vitals: weight, blood pressure, etc.

Medical: medicines, treatments, etc.

Food & nutrition: morning, afternoon, evening (with calories) ...

Exercise: flexibility, cardio, resistance, sports ...

Evening rituals: dinner, family, bed ...

To dos:

Delegated, postponed, declined:

Accomplishments

What, where, when, how, why, who was I today ...

Month _____ Day ___ Year _____

Spiritual: pray, praise, serve ...

Family: love, listen, laugh ...

Friends: reach out, encourage, share ...

Morning rituals: shower, dress, breakfast ...

Vitals: weight, blood pressure, etc.

Medical: medicines, treatments, etc.

Food & nutrition: morning, afternoon, evening (with calories) ...

Exercise: flexibility, cardio, resistance, sports ...

Evening rituals: dinner, family, bed ...

To dos:

Delegated, postponed, declined:

Accomplishments

What, where, when, how, why, who was I today ...

Month _____ Day ___ Year _____

Spiritual: pray, praise, serve ...

Family: love, listen, laugh ...

Friends: reach out, encourage, share ...

Morning rituals: shower, dress, breakfast ...

Vitals: weight, blood pressure, etc.

Medical: medicines, treatments, etc.

Food & nutrition: morning, afternoon, evening (with calories) ...

Exercise: flexibility, cardio, resistance, sports ...

Evening rituals: dinner, family, bed ...

To dos:

Delegated, postponed, declined:

Accomplishments

What, where, when, how, why, who was I today ...

www.ingramcontent.com/pod-product-compliance
Lightning Source LLC
Chambersburg PA
CBHW020448100426
42813CB00026B/3004